FINDING YOU

POEMS AND **REFLECTIONS** FOR THE **JOURNEY** INTO YOUR **SHADOW SELF**

STEVE VINCENT

What people who don't like poetry say about *Finding You*

"Rarely has poetry moved me to tears as those Steve has included in his book, Finding You. These poems, written from Steve's heart, will change your life more than you can imagine. He has an amazing ability to see just what it is we feel and need at different times in our life. Congratulations on a truly inspirational book."

Mama Rae, Healer & Soul Food Chef

"It's so easy to read, and I felt inspired to keep reading. It's raw and heartfelt. You can feel the honesty. I have never enjoyed reading poetry so much and felt it resonated with me. I feel the reflections relate well to the writing and are easy to do."

Deanne Day, CEO

"It's raw, it's real, it's confronting, like you feel naked standing in front of God!"

Sarah-Jane Campbell, Business Development Manager

"I couldn't put it down, and yes, it brought out the tears and helped me reflect on my own journey."

Mark Selbst, Business Coach

"This book is very profound, and it's helped me reach into my shadows where I did not expect to go. Steve's openness and insight are humbling, and his poetry and exercises help you transcend your skeletons and reach a higher state of frequency. Thank you, Steve, for sharing your powerful gift."

Max Koulakov, IT industry

"This book touched me to the core. Steve has poured his heart into these poems and you can feel the depths of his soul in every single word. I am moved by his courage to share so openly. This book is the perfect companion on the human journey to exploring our shadow side and discovering who we REALLY are. It will be your companion in the deepest times of need."

Emily Gowor, Inspirational Writer & Speaker

"I have resonated with so much of this book. Steve's journey into his shadow self reflects much of my own. He has put it all into words - raw, confronting, emotional & painful. He is able to speak out things that for others are just too hard to say. If you are searching for your inner self & are ready to confront your demons, I suggest you dive in, walk with Steve through the shadows & take the opportunity to discover your true authentic self."

Christine Evans, Business Owner

"Raw. Authentic. Emotional. It was just what I needed."

Jenny Harvey, Business Manager

"This touches the heart and makes you want to keep reading, I went through all the emotions and it's comforting to know that I'm not the only one going through this process."

Grace Black, Quantum Healer

Finding You: Poems and reflections for the journey into your Shadow Self
© Steve Vincent 2021

www.stevevincentonline.com

The moral rights of Steve Vincent to be identified as the author of this work have been asserted in accordance with the Copyright Act 1968.

First published in Australia 2021 by Symmetry Marketing and Publishing.

ISBN 978-0-6487841-1-1

Any opinions expressed in this work are exclusively those of the author and are not necessarily the views held or endorsed by Symmetry Marketing and Publishing.

All rights reserved. No part of this publication may be reproduced or transmitted by any means, electronic, photocopying or otherwise, without prior written permission of the author.

Disclaimer

All the information, techniques, skills and concepts contained within this publication are of the nature of general comment only, and are not in any way recommended as individual advice. The intent is to offer a variety of information to provide a wider range of choices now and in the future, recognising that we all have widely diverse circumstances and viewpoints. Should any reader choose to make use of the information herein, this is their decision, and the author and publisher/s do not assume any responsibilities whatsoever under any conditions or circumstances. The author does not take responsibility for the business, financial, personal or other success, results or fulfilment upon the readers' decision to use this information. It is recommended that the reader obtain their own independent advice.

Dedication

This book is dedicated to you... for having the courage to look into your Shadow Self. Many choose to ignore the inner work, to stay stuck and live, as Thoreau said, in quiet desperation. The journey inwards you are about to embark on is your pathway to freedom. It's neither easy nor comfortable nor predictable. Hats off to you...

Preface

I was unhappy. I didn't know why.

Great family. Great home on the water near the beach. Business going well. Happy on the outside, yet unhappy on the inside. WTF? How could this be? Why me? What was going on that I felt this way? ANOTHER mid-life crisis? Did I feel guilty that I felt this way? How could I be unhappy when so many other people had more reasons to be unhappy? Was I depressed? Was I going nuts? Why was my world turning inside and out, and upside down at the same time?

This book is an explanation of, and the answer to, all those questions.

One day when I was feeling pissed off searching for answers and wasn't at work, I sat out the back of my home with a pen and piece of paper. I wrote the words that came to me. I had an urge to make them rhythmic, to make them rhyme. A poem came out. Sounds weird, but in that moment I remembered I had always written poems, even as a teen. But what I had done over the last several decades was shut down the urge to write and create by feeding myself excuses. That it wasn't very manly to write poetry; that my poems were not very good. It was a waste of time. What if people read them and laughed at me? All these thoughts made me close off my heart and ignore that part of my creativity.

My unhappiness that had been building up over the years seemed like the Universe's way of slapping me around, compelling me to dust off those old writing skills. It wasn't that I didn't write and create. I did so every day as a teacher and commercial writer, and to a high level of competency. It was that I didn't write from my truth, from my heart. I wasn't authentically tapping into the God source within. Slap!

Finding You

One of the things that has surprised me about my poems is the response I get. Often, readers say my words, so raw and emotional, have moved them to tears. When I hear that, I realise there is power in writing about my pain and unhappiness. My pain, it seems, is humanity's pain, which is why people connect to it.

And no, this isn't for everyone. Nothing ever is.

The big benefit for me, and it seems for readers of my work, is that these poems encourage us to face our pain, to shine a light on those parts of us we don't want to see or feel.

Having worked through so many of my 'unhappiness issues' via my poems – work, self-worth, family, relationships, parenting, recurring emotional patterns and more – I can say that I'm a much softer, more open and more heartfelt person. That gruff, hard and at times even aggressive shell I wore like a suit of armour is crumbling. I feel more real and alive than I ever have before.

That's not to say that now this book of poems has been published, the journey's over. No way. The journey I've been on, which you witness through these poems, is unpredictable. And it's not easy. Then again, not much in this heavy energy world that is worthwhile is easy.

I encourage you to dive into this book with an open heart and mind. You may even like to gift a copy to someone you feel will benefit from these words. Whether it's for you or someone in your life, the journey ahead in these pages is life changing. It's about deep self-love and it's about finding your real self in all your magnificence, your ugliness, your glory and your pain. Together, let's shine a light on it all so you can begin to love all of you, even those parts you hide from the world.

Let's begin...

Contents

Introduction 1

A Note From An Old Man 10

Can You Hear It? 14

Everything's Fine 18

For You 22

My Ego 26

That Mask You Wear 30

Life Hurts 34

Victory Or Death 38

Apology To My Kids 42

A Message To The Birds 46

The Fog That Surrounds Me 50

Just Be 54

My Prayer 58

Black Shadow Be Gone 62

Just Let Me 66

Because 70

Step Outside 74

Contents

Is It Just Me? 78

I Took A Walk 82

Opposites 83

Affirmations Suck 86

My Old Friend 90

Why 94

I Am 94

Look 94

Believe 94

Bernie 98

Obligation 102

If 106

The Journey 107

They Are All So Happy 110

Reminder 114

Who Are You? 114

Find 114

My Friend Uncertainty 118

When Gaia Talks 122

A Cry For Help 126

The Edge 130

In Hiding 134

The Shift 135

You, The Artist 138

Just 142

Fear 143

It Laughs And Sneers 146

To The Loud Voice 150

Ignore It 150

Release Your Genius 150

You Freak 154

The Search 158

Small Moments 162

Not Two 166

I Am Enough 167

Let Me Flow 170

Am I The Only One? 174

A Brave Young Man 178

This Existence 182

Thoughts 186

Am I Broken? 190

I Needed This 194

I Am Open To... 198

She's Okay, I Think 202

The Guilt Of Religion 206

The Power Of Words 210

The Real You 211

The Cage 214

Contents

The Story Of My Life 218

The Hard-Hearted Man 222

My Attachments 226

Welcome, My Darkest Thoughts 230

Conclusion 234

Acknowledgements 237

About The Author 238

Introduction

The young boy watched the tears run down his mother's face. He felt her pain. And it didn't feel good. This was confusing to him. A five-year-old isn't supposed to have the cares of the world on his shoulders.

But there'd been the car accident that had almost claimed the life of one of his older sisters. His parents did the best they could to shield him from the shock and fear. But he still felt it. And now, they were confronted by another sister's teenage pregnancy. The upstanding Catholic family, the pillar of their community, in turmoil. He felt this too. The embarrassment. The shame. The fear. His mother's tears ran freely as she sniffled, "I'm just so disappointed, she was the smartest of you all."

Yes, he could go off to play in that carefree kid way. And he did. But all this achieved was to squash down the emotions behind her tears deep inside of him, as he pretended they didn't exist.

Then there were the arguments between his father and rebellious older brother. He felt the anger and energy behind these too. To be woken up by loud and harsh male voices was not his favourite start to a day. And the fear and self-loathing other relatives often projected onto the world left him with nervous butterflies having a right old time in his stomach.

This was the 1970s. This was ordinary people doing their best to get by. This was a young boy struggling to understand himself, let alone the world he'd come into.

And the young boy wouldn't realise it until four-plus decades later that he was an empath. A deep feeler and thinker. A sensitive and creative type. It became too difficult for the boy to face these uncomfortable emotions, so he ignored them. He didn't understand why he felt so different.

That doesn't mean his childhood was devoid of care or love. Far from it. Hours riding bikes and playing with neighbourhood kids. Family gatherings and parties. Clean clothes and three lovingly prepared meals each and every day. And his favourite, a glorious beach holiday every year. So yes, his childhood was good, at least to the outside world, and better than many. But it was a tumultuous childhood that left its mark on him. This is not to suggest that anyone went out of their way to do harm. This was normal family life with all its ups and downs. And while he felt every one of them, he often didn't understand the tumult of emotions they spiked in him.

He can't remember the exact moment – some point before he was about ten – when he made a silent pact. He was going to do better. He was never going to cause his parents the pain he felt his older siblings had. It wasn't that he didn't love his siblings. It was that being so soft and caring, he just couldn't do it to Mum and Dad, no matter what the cost to him. It was a brave decision for one so young. But make it he did.

And so it was that the boy embarked on a straight and narrow path, one designed to avoid a repeat of the troubles and turmoil he'd lived through. 'Spikey' emotions he didn't like were stubbornly ignored. No, he didn't want them for himself or for Mum and Dad all over again.

So he set his mind to fulfilling the pact. The walls went up to protect him. And he got to work. He did well academically in primary and high school and then university. He was a competent sportsman as the trophies and certificates attested. He followed the script beautifully. Got a good government job. And before long he married a good Catholic girl and had beautiful kids. He ticked all the right boxes and made Mum and Dad proud, because that was the silent agreement he had made back in the 1970s.

And it fucked him up.

Introduction

That little boy is me, now in my fifth decade. It's not to say my life has been bad. Heck, I've had some fun, travelled the world, achieved career success and made a loving family of my own. But that pact, and all that squashing and rejecting of things I didn't want to see or feel, set in course a life pattern where my Shadow Self was filled to the brim. And it has run my life.

The poems that follow are me facing my Shadow Self. They are raw. They are uncomfortable. And they are deeply personal. My hope is, in exploring my pain, I can encourage you to face those parts of yourself that you have ignored or pushed away because they made you uncomfortable. Maybe you made a similar 'good boy' or 'good girl' pact that led to incessant people pleasing and putting everyone's feelings before your own? Either way, by uncovering, recognising and loving those parts of yourself you have rejected, you can learn to feel better about yourself, to 'find you', so you are at last comfortable in your skin. Wouldn't that be something?

What is the Shadow?

A journey into the Shadow Self is about exploring your demons. Those parts of you that you don't like, have shunned and don't want the world to see. The 'bad' parts you've squashed down and tried to bury. We all have stuff in our Shadow. Jealousy. Feelings of smallness or inadequacy. Shame. Embarrassment. Taboos you secretly like. Ugliness. Anger. Bitterness. Hate. Rage. And more.

The Shadow is those parts of our whole we have repressed because, due to our conditioning from a young age, they make us feel uncomfortable. It's only natural to show the world our 'good' or 'shiny' parts. We all want to be liked. To fit in. And feel 'good'.

Here's the thing though: when we shun and ignore parts of ourselves, they begin to fester. Like the grain of sand that rubs away and turns into the pearl inside the oyster over many years, our 'bad' bits don't go away. Instead, they grow. They can run our lives without us even knowing it. If you've ever felt like a stranger in your skin – no matter how many courses you've bought, how many meditations you've calmed yourself with or how many affirmations you've proclaimed to the Universe – there's a good chance your Shadow runs large chunks of your life. You'll notice this feeling most in times of stress. And if you're a people pleaser or someone who apologises a lot, there's a good chance you will benefit from Shadow work.

The longer we defer facing our Shadow Self, the stronger it grows.

What's the reason for this? I refer here to the work of Dr John Demartini. His teachings describe seven principles that run our lives:

1. Whatever you haven't loved is repeated until it is.
2. Whatever you have not loved runs your life until you do.
3. Whatever you hold back holds you back.
4. Whatever you bury buries you.
5. Whatever you resist persists.
6. Whatever you condemn you breed attract or become.
7. Whatever you infatuate with you undermine.

Read that list again. It's another way of explaining our Shadow or those parts we haven't loved. A wholly loved you – loved by you, that is – vibrates much higher than a you ruled by your Shadow Self.

Facing your Shadow is about claiming your freedom. The freedom to like all of you. And when you do, you feel more flow, more alive and more like you belong, no matter the situation. And when you face life's hurdles after you've done Shadow work, you are okay to speak your truth, and okay with the consequences of speaking your truth.

Introduction

Why else is Shadow Work important?

There is a deeper issue here as well. When you've done Shadow work, you affect those around you.

In his book *The Eye of the I*, Dr David Hawkins reminds us that...

- One person who vibrates at level of optimism and is non-judgmental of others counterbalances the negativity of 90,000 people who calibrate at lower levels.
- One person who vibrates at pure love counterbalances negativity of 750,000 others.
- One person at level of illumination (22 alive today) counterbalances negativity of 10 million.
- One person who vibrates grace counterbalances negativity of 70 million (about 10 people today).

Shadow work helps raise your frequency. When that happens, you affect those around you and the entire planet.

Further, as Rassouli expresses in *Rumi Revealed*:

> *The human being has been formed as the noblest of all creation and the pinnacle of divine expression. Man is life expressed out of the most benevolent love that has ever existed. Yet, he is still walking around in a stupor, unaware of who he is, how elegantly he has been made or how he is created to receive the gift of the fullness of life! Man's challenge is to reach into the depths of his soul to break the hold of the darkness within him. Should anyone choose not to surrender to the divine will, he would not benefit from the gift of this planet or from the gift of life itself.*
>
> *We are summoned as a community of created beings to rise into the fullness of all that we are and to help transform the earth into the paradise of unity it was intended to be.*

So yes, your journey into the Shadow Self is worth it! And so are you.

How Shadow work has affected me

What I can say from doing my Shadow work is that it has changed me as a person. Note, I didn't say I'm now, tah-dah, 'perfect'. I still have human foibles. The key thing, though, is they no longer silently run my life. I don't 'fear' things much at all... work, relationships, speaking my mind, failure, the future. I don't run from things like I used to, in an attempt to 'feel safe'.

Speaking of feelings... now I feel more. My heart isn't closed off behind an iron-clad wall. The 'old me' would never have imagined sharing something so personal like these poems. I mean, how embarrassing! Now? Well, here we are. The old me would have stayed silent to keep the peace. And the old me would have bumbled along passively, a cork on the rough seas of life. Now I steer my own ship. The seas can still be tough at times, but I'm there navigating my way through, from the truth of my open heart. My relationships are getting deeper and more intimate. My life is more a joyous wonder each day as opposed to a battle I hope to struggle through. I'm more open to my moods. More okay with being grumpy and feeling it.

Not only that, I'm prepared to keep looking. When something or someone triggers me, instead of instant harsh judgement of the person or situation, I'm able to look at where that something is in me. Frankly, that's liberating.

It hasn't been easy. I've faced my Dark Night of the Soul and my Valley of Despair. And like you will, I've come out the other side. Because, like you, I'm worth the effort!

How to use this book

I invite you to walk with me. It's a deeply personal journey into friendships, parenthood, relationships with the world, with work and with loved ones. There is pain. There is despair. And there is hope.

When you open the book, you'll find each poem on the left-hand page. After each poem, mostly on the facing right-hand page you will find

Introduction

My Reflections on the poem, or what I was thinking and feeling when I wrote it, plus a number of reflection exercises for you to consider what the words mean for you and space to write what comes to you.

My aim, using the poem as a stimulus, is to prompt something in you and help you look at where it's hiding in your Shadow Self. Stop. Be still. Be authentic with your answers. You're not alone. I'm there too. And it's always comforting to know 'it's not just me'.

You may find the flow from poem to poem messy or chaotic. They certainly are not presented in any chronological order. How can they be? Life is messy and chaotic, as is the journey into our Shadow Self. So you'll find poems about the past, the present and the future.

You may choose to use this book like a novel. Begin at the start and read it all the way through, each poem and reflection in turn. You may like to go with your feelings and just open it to a random page each day. Or something in between. There is no right or wrong.

IMPORTANT: Your Reflections, recorded after each poem, are for your eyes only. This is personal. This is you being honest with you. This is your truth. Share what you discover about you with those closest to you. Or with no one. It's your journey and you have the freedom to choose.

Two more things and a word of caution…

But I can't write very well or I'm not a good writer is BS and not a hall pass to avoid looking deep inside yourself. This is about you. Your responses here are not 'for marks' like in school. So let the words flow. Don't edit as you write, which is hard for the anal types and the Judgey McJudgesons (welcome to the club). Resist the anal editor and let it flow. You don't have to get anything right here. When you write from the heart it is always good enough. Always.

And be alert for blockages lurking where you least expect them. A couple of red flags: *I've already dealt with that* or *I prefer to focus on the positives in life*. These are signs of the conscious mind ignoring the deeper issues in order to keep you safe, because looking deeper can be painful and unpredictable.

When I write now, it's 100% real and from the heart. It's not what I think others might want to read. Not what might sound good to others. Not what will make me look good. That was me a couple of years ago, always worried about what others might think. Now, as you'll see, my writing is raw. It's sometimes about the ugly side of me. And it's sometimes beautiful in what it reveals about me and the human condition. I wish the same freedom for you in these pages.

Good luck. Have fun. Be compassionate to those around you and to yourself.

Take from these pages only that which resonates, leave the rest behind.

Namaste,
Steve

The boys were amazed that I could make such a poem as that out of my own head, and so was I, of course, it being as much a surprise to me as it could be to anybody, for I did not know that it was in me. If any had asked me a single day before if it was in me, I should have told them frankly, no, it was not. That is the way with us; we may go on half a life not knowing such a thing is in us, when in reality it was there all the time, and all we needed was something to turn up that would call for it.

Mark Twain

A NOTE FROM AN OLD MAN

The old man groaned as he sat in his chair
A sharp inward breath, a hand through his thinning hair.
He sighed real deep and gave a weary smile of hope
Took out pen and paper, and here's what he wrote...

To my younger self, when I arrive here next time round
I don't want to be lost, but be a free soul, already found.
Let yourself not worry so much, go on, breathe, smile a lot more
There's fun to be had here if you give up keeping score.

Think with your heart, son, get out of your head
Connect to the real you, enjoy the tears you shed.
Because it's okay to be soft, feel deep, say the unbearable
Your real strength, if you let it, is being true and vulnerable.

You don't have to man up, puff out your chest, a brave BS front
Speak your truth, be real, it's more than just a stunt.
The world will try its best to break you, drag you right down
Stay true to you, feel deep, know that love always abounds.

And there will be times when the path ahead is hard to see
Choose self-honesty always young man, it's the way to be free.
Because those rules, expectations, and judgements damage you slow
Don't get pulled down, they'll try hard to keep you real low.

Hear this loud, you're free to choose in every moment yet
Nothing's chained you up, freedom's yours, don't you forget.
There'll be voices calling, yanking you right off your course
Listen not and when you fall, get up and back on your heart horse.

The world is full of a million fun, shiny, and wonderous things
Let go, dive in, give your all, spread your glorious wings.
Because it's not life playing safe, sitting watching from the fence
All that happens is you shut down, switch off and live life real tense.

When you choose work, hear not what others might say you want
It's your life and lessons, feel them and learn, but stay sane, be nonchalant.
Enjoy it all then, even those spikey, painful, or annoying little bits
Work and contribution are good even if at times it gives you the shits.

But if you live true from your beautiful, strong and pure heart space
Those crappy feelings will never win, let alone keep up the pace.
For when you dance, sing, run and love all anew
It's in those moments you'll see the glory of the real you.

I'm weary from my mistakes, so let me leave you these final thoughts
The heaviness I felt, the weight I carried and the pain they did wrought.
I want that not for you next time round, can't you see?
If only I'd had this letter when I woke up and saw it was me.

MY REFLECTIONS

Regret is a heavy and painful emotion. Pity most of us carry a bagful around with us. When I sat pondering why, these words, through the voice of an old man, came to me.

You see, it's my belief we come here to learn, over many lifetimes, our soul's karmic lessons. If you've ever had a certain situation happen to you over and over again... personality clashes, work situations, family squabbles, to the extent where it becomes a "Oh gosh, not again" for you, there's a good chance there's something buried in your Shadow Self which you haven't looked at and loved. Yet.

Until we do, until we shift the energy trapped there, this pattern repeats and rules our lives. The result is regret. What we should have done. How we should have reacted. Why didn't I do X instead of Y. Know the feeling?

The old man tells us this is normal. But he also leaves a trail of clues about how to deal with it, to the point this is a blueprint of sorts for how to approach our lives.

He wants us to think about what's been before us, so we can better navigate what's ahead of us. He didn't have this letter at the start of his life... but we have it now...

YOUR REFLECTIONS

Reflect on your life to date

What are you most proud of?   What are three things you regret?

1.   1.

2.   2.

3.   3.

If time, money, or life responsibilities weren't a consideration, what "crazy" things would you do? List or draw them here...

What's stopping you? Apart from time, money, or life responsibilities? Be honest here!

CAN YOU HEAR IT?

The gentle heart whispers
The urgent mind shouts
The gentle heart feels
The urgent mind thinks.

The loving heart waits
The fast mind presses
The loving heart is ease
The controlling mind is now.

The vulnerable heart is you
The judging mind is not
The vulnerable heart lasts
The chaotic mind moves.

The peaceful heart feels
The frantic mind pushes
The peaceful heart listens
The frantic mind controls.

The beautiful heart stills
The busy mind grinds
The beautiful heart persists
The busy mind needs.

The soft heart says go slow
The hurried mind says now!
The soft heart is you
The strong mind is only itself.

Who do you listen to...

MY REFLECTIONS

We all have 'voices' in our head. It's normal. At least that's my story and I'm sticking to it!

The thing is, if we haven't done Shadow work, it's likely those negative voices, despite our best efforts, rule our lives.

I have been told by several spiritual teachers that I have a very strong mind. My inner voice is very loud. It often drowns out my heart so much that I can't discern what's the right step ahead.

Have you ever felt this way?

I'm sure it's not just a "guy thing".

I've discovered that to get to my heart space and tap into my inner wisdom, I have to slow down, get still and just be.

As I sat by the water one day I formed words to explain the heart/mind process. This is how it all came out.

Who do you listen to most in your life... your heart or your head...

YOUR REFLECTIONS

List 5 times this week...

	When you felt rushed	When you felt you had plenty of time
1.		
2.		
3.		
4.		
5.		

Now list how you FELT in each moment...

	When you felt rushed	When you felt you had plenty of time
1.		
2.		
3.		
4.		
5.		

Where do you think these feelings have come from?

EVERYTHING'S FINE

You've been lying all this time
The happy, smiling façade in place
But it's numbed you and stopped your shine
No world, I'm okay, everything's fine.

You've been hiding your truth all this time
Nothing to see here, folks, walk on by
It's easier to pretend and toe that line
So they don't see the pain or any other sign.

You've been protecting the shame all this time
The sadness, hurt and guilt kept inside.
Feel the love, friend, time to draw the line
And no, world, everything's not fine.

You've been empty inside all this time
Tears that are trapped, agonizing, unshed.
Release the pain and find your destiny
Listen to your heart, at last, let the true you shine.

MY REFLECTIONS

"Yeah, I'm good, thanks." Ever said that, when someone out of politeness or obligation asks how you are?

When all you want to do, really, is scream at them how shitty you truly feel? Ever felt that? Okay, guess I'm the only one!

This poem is a message from the heart, telling us it's time to be real with ourselves.

No, you don't have to be "good" or "happy" all the time.

It's okay to feel crappy. Or down. Or flat.

And it's definitely okay to speak out your pain.

What is it you really need to say?

Get real and let it flow.

YOUR REFLECTIONS

1. Be honest, raw and real. How do you feel right now in this moment? There is no right or wrong answer!

2. What emotions do you suppress when you're in a group? With your partner? Do you remember the time when you first began doing this? Do you know why you didn't speak out?

3. Pick a moment that triggered you, yet you chose to stay silent. In all your rawness, what would you say now if you had that moment again and weren't concerned with the consequences? Write it down. Use the person's name and be specific...

FOR YOU

This is for you if you don't want to sheep
Like everyone it seems, walking around, fast asleep.

This is for you if you've ever asked why
We're here for a reason, beyond this murky pigsty.

This is for you if you've ever felt all alone
And yearned for the exit to return all the way home.

This is for you if you feel the world's pain
And on your heart it feels like a growing, dark stain.

This is for you if you feel in the minority
While others rush about, bowing to authority.

This is for you if you feel disconnected
The result is a closed heart that needs be protected.

This is for you if you feel stirrings within
And want to scream loud at your sleepy kith and kin.

This is for you if you feel downright confused
The message is simple, time to stand up, stop being used.

This is for you if your heart seeks to be free
The world is ready, go on, come play with me.

MY REFLECTIONS

This is a call to spiritual arms, to 'wake up' even more and take steps on the path you're meant to walk. If I was to shake you spiritually, this is what I would say.

The energy behind this poem rose up during COVID. Frankly, I was horrified at how quickly and easily governments stripped away human rights. Worse, it seemed to me the majority of the population just went along with it all, ne'er a query raised.

And I asked myself, "Am I the only one who feels this way?" The deep disconnect between people and how easily we were divided and manipulated still stuns me.

These words then followed.

YOUR REFLECTIONS

What are your greatest gifts to the world?

Rate how well you use them. Place an 'X' on the scale:

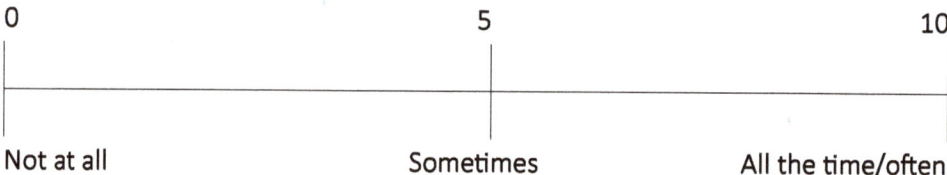

0 — Not at all
5 — Sometimes
10 — All the time/often

Which of these gifts would you most like to pursue? Why?

What's stopping you?

What would a perfect scenario of you using or sharing your gifts with the world look like? Use a series of detailed bullets, or, if you prefer, a free-writing longer monologue.

MY EGO

Why did Ego win battle
After battle?
And rule me for so long?
Why was Ego always
Bossy. Overbearing. Protective.
Needing to win every fight.
Judgement. Fear. Safety.
It drove everything.
And it kept going.
Even when it knew there was a better way.
It made me ignore
Love. Peace. Freedom. Joy.
Hello Spirit. Welcome, at last you're here.
Please stay a little longer.

MY REFLECTIONS

Scientists tell us that every day we have about 50,000 thoughts. About 48,000 of these are Ego thoughts, the rest are Spirit thoughts.

How do you know which is which?

Ego = thoughts of fear, judgement, guilt, anger, immediately, expectation.

Spirit = thoughts of love, peace, joy, happiness, appreciation, forgiveness, patience.

When you stop and 'listen' it can be a little confronting (e.g., *Shit, I have only had one Spirit thought in the last 20 minutes!*).

Monitor your thoughts this week, note when they are the 'spikey' Ego thoughts and how they make you feel… and when they are the gentler but stronger Spirit thoughts and the feelings they stir up in you.

The more you can tip the balance in favour of Spirit thoughts, the more your life changes.

This battle of our mind is what inspired these words.

YOUR REFLECTIONS

How is your mind operating? In Spirit or in Ego? Think back, what were your dominant thoughts this week or month? Make a list below. Don't judge, just observe. Be honest.

EGO THOUGHTS	SPIRIT THOUGHTS
E.g.	E.g.
I was jealous about Mary's Facebook post about her kids' awards	Forgave myself for taking $5 from my sister when I was 7
Got angry at Paul for being late	Felt appreciation as I rode my horse today
Add your own	

If you were in Spirit more often, how would this change your life?

THAT MASK YOU WEAR

Why that mask you wear all through your day?
Is it to cover up what you truly want to say?
Or is the mask a long habit of protection?
To hide your need for deep self-affection?

So why the mask wearing in all that you do?
Maybe it's to hide from the sensitive, real you?
Or is the mask there to keep you sane?
So you never stop and feel the real pain?

Why the mask you work so hard to wear?
Is it to buffer the fear when people stare?
Or is the mask created only in your mind?
When all along it's you you want to find?

Why the mask that hides your true light?
Is it because you're scared to shine bright?
Or is it you just believe all that 3D shit?
When the true beauty in you really is 'it'?

Why this mask you've worn all your life?
Is it just to get by, avoid the emotional strife?
Or maybe it's time to pause and feel not so aloof...
Go on, take it off now and see the beauty of your truth.

Your mask hides your unique genius and power...
So go on, have the courage to remove it this hour...

MY REFLECTIONS

Who is the real me?

The words in this poem came to me as I pondered this question... I reflected how, in every situation every day, I 'showed up' in the world.

Was I 'impeccable' with my word? That is, did the 'real' me present itself? Or was I putting on a front so those around me would like me more?

It goes deeper...

Did the world like the real me... or just the masked version I showed them? Who was the real me? Ouch!

As I pondered this, I realised my purpose on this planet is to help heal humanity through my words.

So I took the commercial writer/business mask off, and what you see here is the result.

Truth bomb: I've worn many masks in my life and I've got to say, I'm not proud of that. Yep, I'm a work in progress. Working on loving my masks.

YOUR REFLECTIONS

Here's a list of the masks we wear. Circle those you wear now or have worn in your life.

The good boy/girl	The good employee
The good religious boy/girl	The good manager
The dutiful and faithful son/daughter	The loving husband/wife
The loving brother/sister	The community contributor
The it'll-be-alrighter	The master coach
The studious student	The good dad/mum
The high achiever	The got-it-all-together dad/mum
The fearful servant	The good bloke
The do-the-right-thing-or-elser	The hard worker
The sport star	The bread winner
The talented professional	The faithful business owner
The worthy-of-love-only-when-you-do-something-worthy	The dutiful, always there, son/daughter and brother/sister... still

How does this realisation make you feel?

Draw one of the masks you wear.

Recall one situation from the last week where you put on a mask. What did you REALLY want to say and do? Write it here. Unmask yourself.

LIFE HURTS

Why does it hurt
When everything seems okay?
Why does it hurt
When everything is so normal?

Why does it hurt
When the day ends?
Why does it hurt
When the day begins?

Why does it hurt
When you win the prize?
Why does it hurt
When you feel so much pride?

Why does it hurt
When you run and hide?
Why does it hurt
And feel so empty inside?

Why does it hurt
When you laugh and have fun?
Why does it hurt
When you're alone in the sun?

Please tell me, why does this life hurt?

MY REFLECTIONS

The Spiritual path in this 3D matrix is never easy to tread. Do you walk around with pain? It may be emotional. Or it could manifest in the physical. Have an honest look... where are you in pain?

The reason I ask is that one day as I sat down to journal, I felt really pissed off. I had no idea why. Looking at my life it all seemed good. Business was doing well. Nice home. Cars. Good marriage and good kids. What had I got to complain about? My rational mind tried to dismiss the ructions in me... *it's not that bad... what are you talking about... others are worse off...* and on it went.

Rationally, everything was fine. Yet I wasn't. Maybe it was Divine Discontent. Maybe it was the Dark Night of the Soul. I'm not sure, to be blunt.

If you've ever felt this way too, these words may resonate.

YOUR REFLECTIONS

Take an inventory of your physical and emotional pains. The energy always comes out in the body. Reach out into each one and feel it... where does it come from?

Physical Inventory	Emotional Inventory
E.g. Headache – worrying about the bills	E.g. Angry from a disagreement with supervisor at work, felt unfairly treated

Recall a time when you were happy and free like a child. Write this out... Where were you? What sounds and smells do you remember? Who was you with? What brought you so much joy? How did it feel?

When did you lose this child-like freedom? What would it mean to you to get it back?

VICTORY OR DEATH

Victory or death, their energy said unto me
Slay them, beat them, you'll stay safe can't you see?
It's the only way to get by, victory at all costs
Even when you follow this path it becomes a life lost.

All your communications must be this forceful way
What else is there but to show 'em and win the day?
Victory is sweet, you walk away on top
Even if all you've done is make your heart drop.

But lead on, forward still into the breach
Be on guard, school them up, these ones there to teach.
Coz it's your role here and now to feel all superior
Win that argument, these mere plebs, my they are inferior.

It's a stellar win you seek in every situation
Victory or death comes without moderation.
They can't possibly be right, you're the hero and king
Go on, get out there, knock 'em dead, do our thing.

Take the W and hang all the expense
Don't realise, all-out victory is but a mere fence.
You hide behind it foolishly, so you never get hurt.
C'mon mind, here's another chance, stay alert.

If only they'd taught it's the heart that really counts
To be true, alive, free, not on guard, ready to pounce.
So I go through life, guns up ready for battle.
Victory after victory is but my soft heart's death rattle...

MY REFLECTIONS

It took 50+ years for me to finally figure out how and why I communicate the way I do (or don't). That's how it was in my younger years from those around me... a victory or death mentality in every communication.

The hard part is, when that's all you know... well, that's all you know. Disagreements with my siblings as kids and as adults always ended in bitterness with a clear winner and loser. In fact, I don't recall us ever sitting down to talk or it being okay to say how I really felt, without judgement.

This poem reveals what it's like. Maybe you had a similar experience growing up? Maybe yours was completely the opposite? If so, this may explain why some people in your life are the way they are.

Either way, this poem challenges us to reflect on how we communicate now, and confront how we were taught to communicate growing up or how we now deal with differing views.

YOUR REFLECTIONS

What was your family's communication style? List words or phrases that describe it.

Do you wear masks when you communicate? What are they? E.g., the peacemaker, the go-along-with-them-to-avoid-pain nice guy/girl? List them.

How do you feel about the realisation you may have worn a mask at times in your life?

Do you bite your tongue? List three examples of when you have. What would you have said if you were being 100% honest in the moment?

APOLOGY TO MY KIDS

To my darling children, whom I love so very much,
I still can't believe the universe gifted me with your luck.
But as I've gotten older and learned more about life,
I may have caused you pain, even emotional strife.

Because I fear I've used you for my own ego ends,
Not let you be free to change, to learn and to bend.
I wanted us all to look good for the world to see,
When all I've done is stifled you, stopped you being free.

All my rules, conditions, the way things HAD to be,
It pains me deeply, only now I've found the happiness key.
And I fear it's too late now, the damage has been done,
I'm so sorry to squash you, keep you from your sun.

You shine bright in the world more than I ever did,
Too scared to be seen, I really just ran and hid.
If I projected this fear onto your beautiful clear soul,
I'm ashamed that I have, quick, dig me a hole.

So please, forgive my failings as your lucky dad,
It wasn't intentional, I want our time together re-had.
Because the agony I feel now, I held you too closely
And polished you up to be my ego world trophy.

And this bullshit on you is heavy, horribly unfair,
I hate what I've done, it drives me to despair.
All those conditions were just part of my biology,
It matters not now, please accept this, my humble apology…

MY REFLECTIONS

My child isn't my easel to paint on.

Nor my diamond to polish.

My child isn't my trophy to share with the world.

Nor my badge of honour.

My child isn't an idea, an expectation, or a fantasy.

This quote from Dr Shefali Tsabury is what inspired this poem. It prompted me to ask: Where have I made my kids a 'trophy'? How have I 'polished' them up to shine in the world as a reflection of me? Did these actions, over so many years, serve my ego or my child's higher good?

This is a VERY difficult question to be honest with yourself about.

For me it's confronting. It brought up great sadness because it made me realise there were times when I had turned them into a trophy of sorts.

More importantly, it made me realise, like I said in the introduction, that I had agreed to be a trophy to my parents so they would avoid more pain.

For me, this is the saddest poem in the collection. Even though I wrote it and have read it many times, it still spikes my emotions, and a tear threatens to show itself whenever I read it.

YOUR REFLECTIONS

List ways you have placed expectations on your children. If you don't have kids, where do you see this in how others parent?

Did your parents make you their trophy? How does this make you feel? Write your thoughts here...

If you feel compelled to, write a letter of apology to your kids.

What feelings came up for you?

A MESSAGE TO THE BIRDS

To fly like a bird in the skies, forever free
Chirping away loud as you like, happy for others to see
Or to soar like the sea eagle, majestic and high
Oh to let go and roam like that, it makes my heart sigh.

To swoop down and rest or just sit and be still
To do whatever you feel must be a great thrill.
You start each day with a happy bright song
And gather together in a spirited noisy throng.

Every day it seems you have it all together
Able to flow and thrive, no matter the weather.
You're nimble and light in every single way
Oh to be that clear, it must be the happiest day.

But you do it all the time, all through the seasons
Never it seems weighed down by your demons.
Liberty is your birthright to fly up high aloft
Your heart must be pure, so happy and soft.

So you may be tiny and not so significant
But you have much to teach this here 3D variant.
Because I watch you flit, fly, and wish I were so
But my search goes on, my battle rages to and fro.

Please keep showing up, my little feathered friend
You inspire my quest which never seems to end.
But just being there happy, light, and free
Helps me find those qualities buried deep inside me.

MY REFLECTIONS

I love to sit in my backyard, especially early mornings and late afternoons. The birds – from the tiny but feisty Willy Wagtail to the fast and diving seagull to the magnificent soaring Sea Eagle – they show up every day in their unique way.

The thing is they rarely seem to change. They just keep on keeping on, happy in their skin to do their thing. They seem so confident and self-assured, no matter their differences. They seem to not have a care in the world despite the weather, the changes to their environment. They are just themselves. I admire this. It seems a perfect way to be.

So one day I asked Spirit what message the birds had for me. This was the answer.

YOUR REFLECTIONS

Sit in nature. Have a conversation with a bird. Or a tree. Or the wind. What messages did you receive?

If you were free like a bird, where would you go? What would you do? Really let go and see what comes to you...

What 'you' qualities have you buried? What's stopping you releasing them?

THE FOG THAT SURROUNDS ME

I open my eyes to the familiar soup-like fog
It surrounds me, that feeling of deep brain clog.

Lost in my home, can't see where to turn,
The numbness, the void, my soul it does burn.

Next day there is sun, bright and clear to see,
Oh Creator Spirit, this is it, why can't it always be?

And I'm happy at last, till the fog comes over again,
A trigger I know not, the fog it will descend.

Where did my vision, power and happiness go?
Lost to the fog, swallowed up and gone, wish it weren't so.

So I trudge on and on, smile empty at passers-by,
They too lost in this goop, they too don't know why.

A ray of sun, oooh, again it beams down, offers more hope,
Then the fog returns, a life-long game of rope-a-dope.

How to break this cycle, bring light to melt the fog away,
It's the question I ask, morning, night, and all through my day.

And looking within, speaking out emotions that hurt so
Lifts the fog just a little, gives me less angst, less to and fro.

At least now the path ahead has opened up just a little more,
And melted the goop that surrounds, a chance for peace to restore.

MY REFLECTIONS

Some days I feel like shit. Down. Dark. Broken. At least now, through my words, I'm ok to admit it and not force the happy mask in place.

I renounce all claims to being 'the nice guy' just to please others. I refuse to smile for the photo. When I'm pissed off, I own it and welcome it. This up and down, this to and fro, this is me.

Yes, some days it feels like I'm surrounded by a fog, and I don't know why. What I've learned is that it's most important to simply accept it, not fight it.

If you've ever felt cheesed off and don't know why, you're not alone. These words may help you realise it's okay.

YOUR REFLECTIONS

Where in your life can you be more open or authentic?

How has hiding how you really feel benefited you?

How has it hurt you?

What else came up for you in reading this poem?

JUST BE

Let go
Open up
Be still
Find quiet
Just be.

Turn off
Shut down
Allow in
Slow time
Just be.

Go soft
Lighten up
Feel love
Release tension
Just be.

Close eyes
Shrug shoulders
Silence mind
Welcome calm
Just be.

Feel good
Hold space
Listen out
Feel free
Just be.

Sit there
Look around
Listen up
Breathe deep
Hello me.

MY REFLECTIONS

When was the last time you sat and let yourself 'just be'? In our fast-paced world, this kind of self-care is vital. After all, how can you possibly get to know yourself and your Shadow Self if you don't take the time to look?

I've gotten better at it, but I've still got a long way to go. If I let my mind race, there's always something to do or some place to be.

Just stop. Just be still with yourself. Just be.

When you do, magic can happen in terms of solutions to challenges you may be facing, new ideas or the greatest gift of all... a still mind. Even if it's just for a short period of time, a free and still mind is a beautiful thing to help your inner light shine.

YOUR REFLECTIONS

Time yourself – 5 minutes… sit there, just be. When the timer's up, note down below whatever came up for you.

What blocks you from 'just be' moments?

What does 'just being' look like to you? Describe or sketch your ideal place to 'just be'...

MY PRAYER

And so today, right now, time seems to stand still.
Yoga calms. Heals. Uplifts. Slows time.

Why is this different to other days?
The vagaries of life and our inner world.

To be this. Timeless. Unhurried. Free. Calm. Alive.
The wonder of this moment. If only I could bottle it.

Great Creator, I ask your assistance to help me slow time.
To feel from the heart. To live in the heart.

I hand it all over to you... every outcome, every result, every thing.
Business. Love. Life. Everything.

Thank you. I trust in you to bring me my highest and
best good in every moment.

Amen.

MY REFLECTIONS

After yoga one day, I sat out the back and examined how I felt. Did the yoga benefit me? Would I be better off sleeping in? Going to the gym? Going for a walk?

This poured out. Yes, the coffee tasted extra good too. I prefer a piccolo because I don't like a lot of milk. On that day I really enjoyed it – it seemed my prayer was answered.

One other point: this poem is about our attachments to what we believe to be the 'right' outcome for us. It's important to realise that our egos don't know so much and certainly can't comprehend all possibilities.

Go ahead, slow time....

Let go of fixating on the outcome of what might come to you...

YOUR REFLECTIONS

If you feel compelled, write your own prayer in the space below. How are you feeling? What would you ask assistance with? There's no right or wrong here.

BLACK SHADOW BE GONE

Stop checking up, I'm okay right now,
Your shadow is there this and every hour.
All these years you've watched over me
There to judge, manipulate, ensure others see.

You always checked up, there all the day,
Ever watching over, monitoring what I say.
Day in day out, never a moment's peace,
There to control, subdue, make me feel least.

You're here right now making sure this verse rhymes,
What I really want to say is, 'Just fuck off!'
Ha! I said it with no thought to convention,
And fuck, it felt good, no apprehension.

Why must you harass and badger me so,
Isn't there enough pain, you need to let go?
So just fuck off and leave me well alone,
Let me be free, it's my own journey home.

Here's one last verse for you to oversee,
Your shadow is fading, it's the real me.
And when you at last cease to poke and exist,
Black Shadow be gone is my greatest conquest.

MY REFLECTIONS

There have been times in my life when it felt like I was being 'watched'. Or at least many of my thoughts would go through a 'is this the right thing to do' filter. So it felt like there was a presence hovering, judging my every move, like a dark shadow.

Here's what I've come to realise... if there is a darkness there hovering over you, it's darn hard for your light to shine.

If you've ever felt this, you will resonate with these words.

Let's shine a light on the black shadow in this now moment...

YOUR REFLECTIONS

When are you critical of yourself? What does the voice say? Pick at least three times you were aware of this voice, and note down here what it was saying to you.

How does this voice make you feel?

What thoughts would you prefer to dominate your mind? How would this change your life?

JUST LET ME

Just let me walk my path with ease
Just let me walk my path with peace.

Just let me feel safe and okay within
Just let me hear above the worldly din.

Just let me see the best thing for me
Just let me align, a servant to thee.

Just let me have some hours pain free
Give me space, please, just to be me.

Just let me have a day, without a worry
Just let me live with ne'er a sorry.

Just let me be okay to speak my truth
Just let me be okay to hit the fucking roof.

Just let me sit and do nothing at all
Just let me live and not have to call.

Just let my mind be still and blank
Just let me pause and refill my tank.

Because I can't keep going like this
The turmoil, pain and hurt has me in fits.

Just let me feel that real true thing
Just for today, let my artist's heart sing.

MY REFLECTIONS

Have you ever felt like you've had enough? That you just want to tell the world to shove it?

I have. Only once, I swear!

One day it hit me particularly hard. I'd had enough of all the trivial things, all the moderate mediocre things, and all the big things. The whole lot.

I just wanted to be left alone in peace without all this stuff going on.

So I did what I often do when there's an emotional spike like this…

I got out my journal, went outside, tapped into the emotions and put the pen to paper.

Here's what came to me…

YOUR REFLECTIONS

RESPOND TO THE FOLLOWING:

1. I am most creative when:

2. What I really love about me is:

3. My creativity feels blocked when:

4. If time, supposed talent or money weren't obstacles, I'd get creative and I'd... (be as detailed and descriptive as possible):

EXTRA NOTE: Take 30 minutes every day to do something that energises you and feeds your creativity. EVERY day. Write. Journal. Walk in nature. Paint. Colour in. Play guitar. Dance. Sing. Act out a scene from a favourite play. Read aloud from a novel or a piece of your own writing you love. Just do it. EVERY day.

BECAUSE

Why are you so grumpy today, they asked.
Because I am, I said.

Why are you so jealous of her, they inquired.
Because I am, I said.

Why do you have to speak like that, they blurted.
Because that's how I feel, I said.

Why are you so quiet today, they wanted to know.
Because I am, I said.

Why are you sad when you hear that, they begged.
Because I am, I said.

Why don't you laugh louder like them, they mused.
Because I don't feel like it, I said.

Why are you pissed off at him, they prodded some more.
Because I am, I said.

Why are you now dancing and singing, they poked again.
Because I am, I said.

Why are you so up and down, they pushed further still.
Because I'm real and that's how I feel, I said.

Go on, be your truth and feel it, let it out.
Because you are real.

And you are okay.

MY REFLECTIONS

Just keep the peace, hey? Been there, done that for far too much of my life.

These words came to me following a discussion about the Dark Feminine energy. In particular, how she suppresses others and stops you feeling. Yes, it's about the mask you wear. But it's also about WHY you wear the mask.

Is it okay to be yourself with all your pain and faults and craziness? Or do you keep the peace just to make things 'easier'? Remember, energy can't be destroyed, only moved... if you keep it locked away, it comes out eventually.

Love all of yourself, even the bits others may find awkward. See the last line for why!

YOUR REFLECTIONS

Do you wear the 'mask of niceness'? List 5 times when you did:

1.

2.

3.

4.

5.

What did the mask 'cost' you? Dig deep here...

Thinking back to the masks you identified in the first reflection, how will you approach the situation differently in the future? How will this make you feel?

STEP OUTSIDE

Hold on tight, keep that lid there shut,
Safety first, stay inside that protective hut.

Everything in here's so comfy and familiar
Out there it's tough, might even kill ya.

Outside is wild, unknown, and uncertain.
Go on, have a peek, move aside that curtain.

They're out there playing, getting dirty and hit
Stay safe in here, you don't need that shit.

Because you're not like them, you're alone in here,
Even if this regret, held tight, is too much to bear.

At least in here you know what you face every day,
But what would it be like to go outside and play?

Seems scary, have to face stuff I don't want to see,
The realisation, perhaps, out there is the real me.

I've been programmed to play things all too safe.
Hurry up, get ready, you can't be late.

But to stay in here is to waste my life force,
Go on, I dare you, step out, get on that horse.

Staying inside is but a mere form of 'be',
It's out there when you venture, you truly find free.

MY REFLECTIONS

Like you, I've achieved much in my life. And like I've said already, I have all the outward signs of a successful life.

But one question nags at me… have I really 'dived in'?

In other words, have I taken enough risks? Have I really let go and sucked the marrow out of life? Or have I played it safe? What do I hold onto or don't want to lose? What is my 'pattern'? Where am I ruled by fear?

I pondered these questions one day sitting by the ocean. What came to me was two images. Was I the scared little boy inside looking out the window watching other kids play, too timid to join in? Or was I out there, jumping and running and yelling and having fun without a care in the world?

Which one are you?

YOUR REFLECTIONS

If there were NO impediments (money, time, access, relationships), what 5 things would you really like to do in your life?

What emotional blocks have stopped you from doing these 5 things?

What would your life be like if you didn't give two fucks about what others thought of you and what you did? How would that feel? Make notes in the space below:

IS IT JUST ME?

Is it just me, or does this feel surreal
Like a dream to disown and forever seal?
Is it just me, or does the knocking just keep
While everyone else walks along in a deep sleep?

Is it just me, or has it all come on at once?
Wake up, people, don't act like the clueless dunce.
Is it just me who wants to gawk and stare
At all the injustice, rules, coercion, that's unfair?

Is it just me who feels this deep-seated anger
Because it seems our freedom's in grave danger?
Is it just me who hungers for lots more
For a world that's not about just keeping score?

Is it just me who wants to rip off the shackles
But feels the weight of raising others' hackles?
Is it just me who wants to go and dig deep
And really know me, but is scared, afraid to weep?

Is it just me who feels all this deep internal pain
Attached, it seems, to every sinew, on my heart a stain?
Is it just me who wants to fly home?
Not stay here, I'm bored, living like a drone.

Is it just me who craves a deeper truth
But balks all the time searching for proof?
Is it just me who carries layers of shame
When all I want really, is to not feel the pain?

MY REFLECTIONS

I feel different from others. At least, that's the way it seems to me. Not necessarily better or worse, just different. Ever had the same thought?

Now I'm not sure if it's true or if I'm just a little weird, but it kind of feels right. For starters, not everyone bares their soul in a book of poems.

So if you've ever felt alone or weird or different, this poem is for you. If you want to break out and scream "fuck you!" to the world, this poem is for you. Or if you want to dive deeper into who you really are, yes, this poem is for you.

Good to have another fellow weirdo onboard!

YOUR REFLECTIONS

Write a love letter to yourself. Be gentle. Include understanding, acceptance and self-care.

Dear

I TOOK A WALK

I took a walk with love
And time stood still.

I took a walk with love
And felt for a moment, free.

I took a walk with love
And let go of the heavy 3D.

I took a walk with love
And felt for a moment, peace.

I took a walk with love
And felt a giant release.

I took a walk with love
And wandered by the sea.

I took a walk with love
And found the real me.

OPPOSITES

Power in weakness
Strength in vulnerability
Open your heart
And see the real you.

Passion in peace
Movement in stillness
Open your heart
And feel the real you.

Action in the quiet
Life in the moment
Open your heart
And connect to the real you.

MY REFLECTIONS

Yin/Yang. We live in a world of duality. Sunny days, rainy days. Good moods, bad moods. The thing is, nature always finds a balance. Why then do I feel unbalanced? How do I fit in?

And when life gets busy, how do I slow down?

My struggle to 'fit in' to this world is expressed in these two poems.

Taking a walk is one thing that helps. Being honest with myself is another. For example, all the opposites in our world can be truly baffling. Sometimes I feel confused and lost.

Have you felt this way too?

YOUR REFLECTIONS

Take a walk. Concentrate on your steps, on your surroundings. When you get home, note down what came up for you. Be honest!

What feelings does the word 'opposites' bring out in you now?

AFFIRMATIONS SUCK

How can they work...
Their positivity
Their emotion
Their niceness
Their encouragement?

How can that work...
When you don't FEEL
One tiny part of what they say?

'I am happy and abundant'
Repeat it all day

Nuh. Makes no difference
When I FEEL
Broken, empty, poor.

Just hollow words that make you a hypocrite.
But they drink the cool aide and lap this stuff up.

Yes, affirmations suck.
There, someone had to say it...

MY REFLECTIONS

I've tried just about everything. Positive sayings. Subliminal meditations. Affirmations plastered on walls. You name it, I've had a crack. They worked for a while. Or seemed to.

What really happened, I believe, is that they distracted me for a short period of time. But they did nothing to address the Shadow.

For me, using affirmations is like, *just by saying these nice things the ugly or uncomfortable parts of me will – hey presto! – disappear.*

It doesn't work, at least for me.

Yep, I get pushback from others for saying affirmations suck. Maybe I'm just built different.

But someone had to say it!

YOUR REFLECTIONS

How do you feel about affirmations? Have you got any favourites? How long have you used them? What 'positive things' have you tried (courses, meditations, journaling, etc.)? How did it all work out for you? What challenges do you still face? Record your answers here...

MY OLD FRIEND

Hello old friend,
Great to see you again.
You're back one more time,
Trying to make amends?

You've been with me so long,
I can't even remember.
Always there to help,
And feel like you belong.

What would my life be like
Without you there always?
It would be different, yes,
Maybe I'd love me more, despite?

Like a pain I feel you, yes,
Poking, prodding, watching,
Ever reminding me so
Here today and tomorrow, bless.

The last time I let you go
You begged to come back
I resisted you some
You're still here, it is so.

How to let you go, you're so well built
All through my life there,
In every moment, loyal
Your name is familiar, hello guilt.

MY REFLECTIONS

This is a big one for me. I'm a work in progress, loving and embracing the guilt I carry. But it's there, a hard habit to break. This is multi-layered in me. Catholic guilt. Guilt used as a tool to manipulate me as a kid so I toed the line. Guilt when I was happy. Guilt when I was sad. It's been like a life-long unwanted companion. This poem is about acknowledging, welcoming and loving this part of my Shadow.

Is there a nagging part of you that feels uncomfortable, which you don't want to look at? If yes, it's okay. You have to first be ready to look at it. It took me 50 years to see it, and another couple to really love it. Just look, that's a start.

YOUR REFLECTIONS

Which emotion is like your old friend? From your earliest memory, why did you reject it and push it back into your shadow?

Write a thank you note to the emotion you just identified. How has hanging on to that emotion served you?

If your 'old friend' emotion had a colour or a face, what would it be? Draw it here...

WHY

Why is it so hard to trust?
Why does my mind rule my heart?
Why is it so easy to see lack?
Why does my mind drag me down?
Thinking. Analysing. Fearing.
Wanting. Striving.
Why can't I just find peace?

I AM

I am, that I am.
Here now... one of my lives.
Same soul...
Different place, different time.
But the same beautiful soul journey through the ages.
Loving. Free. Empowered.
I am, that I am.

LOOK

Look inside to find the answers.
Look inside to find peace.
Look inside to find abundance.
Look inside to find your power.
Look inside to find the divine.
Look inside to find love.

BELIEVE

Believe in love,
It starts inside.
It then radiates out
And touches everything and everyone.
Just start with and return to love.
That is the answer.

MY REFLECTIONS

While I prefer longer poems, there are times when short ones pop up like surprises. These poem-ettes, like I call them, just came to me same as normal words do. The difference is, they stopped after one verse. Why? I have no idea!

It's a weird thing, this writing. The hardest part is starting out, just letting the pen or keyboard flow. The second hardest part is ending, or knowing when to end. These poems broke the rules. And I kind of love them for it.

They reflect what was in me at the time of writing them. They were penned months apart; they just started and then stopped, complete in themselves.

YOUR REFLECTIONS

What do these poem-ettes stir up in you? Respond in whatever way feels most appropriate to you. Add a couple more verses, write your own, list random thoughts, sketch, turn one into a song... You will know what to do.

BERNIE

It's just so unfair, the timing is all wrong
I'm stuck in this pain where I just don't belong.

It's just so unfair, you're tired, leaning on the post
My rock and my strength, it's now I need you most.

It's just so unfair, there's so much still to do
I want you beside me to see this one through.

It's just so unfair, you've given us so much
I didn't realise, truly you're my emotional crutch.

It's just so unfair, how guilty I now do feel
You fading fast was never part of our deal.

It's just so unfair, how I yearn, at times so alone
When all along you worked your fingers to the bone.

It's just so unfair, that no one else can see
The pain that I carry that stops me being free.

It's just so unfair, how the cards have been dealt
We don't deserve this, it makes my heart melt.

It's just so unfair, this path that lay ahead
I fear walking it alone, the tears I must shed.

It's just so unfair, the way my world's turning
Stick with me some more, my darling Bernie.

MY REFLECTIONS

A dear friend, a tad older than me, had the courage to visit her Shadow Self. One of the fears that came up for her was her husband of four-plus decades declining and/or passing away, leaving her alone to face the toughest emotional challenges in her life.

The day after our conversation, I wrote this poem. I cried when I finished, because it brought up how fragile life is and why now, in this very moment, is the BEST time to start looking at your Shadow and walking the path to freedom.

Like this poem says, while you're on the path, expect a tear or two. Plus, you never know where it will end up taking you, so I encourage you not to cling to a certain outcome.

YOUR REFLECTIONS

What fears about your life or closest relationships do you secretly harbour? Make a list.

Pick one fear from the list above. Take some time to love the part of you that fears this happening. Give it a hug. Record what you felt in the space below.

Now speak it out loud.

How do you feel about that fear now?

OBLIGATION

I should.
I must.
I have to.
I'm sorry.
Please.
Thank you.
I apologise.
Be good.
Do the right thing.
Maybe I should just be.
Let go.
Trust.
Love.
Just be.
Maybe I should... just be.
And let it all unfold.
In divine right timing.
Yes, the truth...
I should just be.

MY REFLECTIONS

The honest, real, raw me hates expectations. Doing things just to please others is a mini death sentence, because you subjugate your needs and free will to someone else's. That sucks.

One day I was feeling pretty crappy after I'd agreed to a request from a friend. I pondered why. It's good to give, to help others, right? As I tapped into the root of my feeling, I realised it was because I didn't want to do it and had only said yes to be nice. I wasn't being true to myself. And this made me ponder this insidious force in my life and how it has ruled me for so long. Here's what came out...

Oh, and one other thing that came out was 'no more'. My obligation is to me. This doesn't make me a bad person. It merely rights the ledger of this lifetime.

YOUR REFLECTIONS

Obligations produce a winner and a loser. Think about your life. Be raw and honest here. List 10 obligations that come to you. Don't judge these, or the other people involved or yourself. Just list them.

Re-read your list. What emotions came up?

Take back your power now. List three obligations. Beside each, note how you can change these, so you aren't the 'loser' in the interaction anymore. 'Stop it' is a valid answer.

Remember to love the obligation in you.

IF

If you haven't got time, take just ten minutes now.
If you haven't got ten minutes, take an hour now.
If you haven't got an hour, take half a day.
If you haven't got half a day, take a weekend.
If you haven't got a weekend, take a week.
If you are rushed, tired, stressed, anxious...
Take time alone now and connect to the real you.
Do it today.

THE JOURNEY

It doesn't have to make sense.
Trust.
Allow.
Let go.
Yes, act.
Motion beats meditation.
But...
Trust.
Allow.
Let go.
Because...
Spirit has your back.
And...
Right now...
It doesn't have to make sense.
Let go.
Let the journey unfold
In divine right timing.

MY REFLECTIONS

I never have enough time to... fill in the blanks. We all have our 'wish I could' list. It seems the older we get, the more tech we use, and the more media we consume, the faster our pace of life becomes. I dislike this rush, the feeling that there's never enough time. I make it a point to reclaim some time each day and be still. These two poems are a tribute to the need for stillness in my life.

If = my life has been so driven by deadlines... too much rushing, my mind too busy. Have I really been 'present' and enjoyed the moments? Does this hit a nerve in you?

The Journey = I've never trusted life enough. This is my declaration of intent. I'm a work in progress!

Sit. Be still. Breathe.

YOUR REFLECTIONS

"If"

Rate your current ability to take time out.

1   2   3   4   5
○   ○   ○   ○   ○

List three things you can do this week to change your busy habits.

1.

2.

3.

"The Journey"

Do you hold on too tight to an outcome? Is force or flow more your modus operandi? What came up for you when you read this poem? What parts of you do you need to love?

1.

2.

3.

THEY ARE ALL SO HAPPY

*Searching. No answers. Nothing. Empty.
Why is this life so hard? Everyone else seems so happy, they do it easy.
Nothing interests me. Nothing excites me.
Nothing shifts. It's the same pain each day.
It was here yesterday. It is here today.
It will probably be here tomorrow too.*

*This spinning wheel of despair. When will it stop?
A lifetime of discipline. Some success. At least on the outside.
But really, just the same wheel spinning.
Why? Not the right path?*

*Are there internal blocks? But I've done the work. Read the books.
Resistance. Comfort in pain. Afraid of joy... it's for someone else.
There's no time. There's no time for fun. Or love. Or relaxation.
Too much human doing. Not enough human being.
Another mountain to climb.*

*What brings joy? Who really knows anymore?
Is this shit all there is?
It's not money. It's not fame. It's not even impact.
It's just within... and it's empty.
Do others feel this way? Or just me?
What's wrong with me?
Why is there no peace after all this time...
all this money... all this effort?*

Why? Why? Why?

MY REFLECTIONS

I'm not a huge fan of social media. At times it feels like narcissism on a screen. *Look at my holiday. Look at my scraped knee. Look at me smiling at my success. Look at me, I'm sooo excited to be at this event/party.*

Why does this trigger me? Am I not happy? Why aren't I happy more often? Are others happier than me, like they show on social media so often? Am I the only one who feels like this? Am I just a little bit broken? Or maybe I'm just a grumpy, moody prick...

YOUR REFLECTIONS

Respond to each of the following:

I'm happiest when...

I'm at my darkest when...

I get annoyed when...

I love it when…

How do you feel, honestly, when you see other's success, even someone you dislike?

Select one of your answers above. Speak it out now.

REMINDER

There is much love for you here.
You are amazing.
You are brilliant.
Rest in the peace and love of Spirit.
Open your heart.
Heal.
Believe.
Let go.
Open up.
Love.
Feel from the heart...
That's where it counts.

WHO ARE YOU?

Do you really know me?
Do I really know me?
Do you like what you see?
Do I like what I see?
...I don't actually know...
Is it time to recall who I am...

FIND

Find my heart
Find my voice
Find myself
Find my path
Find my love
Find me.

MY REFLECTIONS

Some more poem-ettes. Again, I didn't set out for brevity. They just turned out that way. The journey into the Shadow can feel very negative, heavy and dark. It helps to keep perspective.

Here are my thoughts around each:

Reminder is, well, a reminder that all is not horrible. When you journey into the Shadow it can feel like you're going nuts. You're not. You're only shifting energy, which causes an unsettling in your field. Like purging in an ayahuasca ceremony, *this too shall pass.*

Who Are You: Sometimes while journeying into the Shadow, it can feel like you don't know yourself anymore. I felt this way one day and when I asked what was going on, these words came out.

Find: This is my quest!

YOUR REFLECTIONS

What came up for you reading these three short poems?

If you were to sketch your answer to the above question, what would it look like? Draw it below.

MY FRIEND, UNCERTAINTY

I ignored you all these years
I ran from you, it drove me to tears

You were anything but safe
See, I never wanted to be late.

Yet there you were anyways
And in you magic was present, always.

But I looked the other way
And stuck real hard I did stay.

When I embraced you it felt good, frequently
You my lifelong and faithful friend, uncertainty.

I embrace you now, welcome your gifts
I thank you now, help me make the shift.

Time to take that leap of faith with
You, my friend, the great uncertainty.

MY REFLECTIONS

This is more how I want to be, than who I have been. Much of my life has been ruled by fear – fear of the unknown, of failure, of looking small in front of others. Such fear can be paralysing.

I wrote this one following a conversation with a friend who runs a hedge fund that deals in millions of dollars of other people's money EVERY day. As we were talking about the possibility of the success of a certain project we were working on, I defaulted to my 'sounds risky' fear-based paradigm. His response hit me like a punch in the guts: "Steve, everything in life is a risk. If we don't risk anything, we achieve nothing." Ouch.

As I work with the Shadow, I let go more and embrace uncertainty, not cling to a predetermined outcome that feels safe. The more and more I do this, the better it feels. And the freer I become.

YOUR REFLECTIONS

Do you play small in your life? Do you hold back because you're unsure of the outcome? List areas in your life below where this is the case. Next to each, explore why. Make sure you note down what emotions come up for you.

WHEN GAIA TALKS

The wind blows
And we don't hear it.
We're too busy rushing
Doing, striving, pushing.

The clouds roll in
And we don't even look up.
There's money to be made
Bills to pay, trinkets to acquire.

The waves curl over and crash down
But rarely do we see
We don't stop in awe
We walk on to the next thing.

The rain trickles down
Yet we have to get it all done
We don't marvel at the life it brings
Because there's important stuff to do.

The majesty of life
In faith goes on around us
We're too busy and frantic to slow and care
And this is why we're unhappy inside, see?

MY REFLECTIONS

I love being in nature – the beach, the rainforest, the water. It struck me one day when I was alone paddling in a creek, to wonder if people really take the time to listen and connect to Mother Earth or appreciate the beauty around us. My guess, sadly, is that the answer for many is no. All our electronic devices dull our senses and appreciation of the majesty of our planet.

When I returned home from my paddle, this is what I wrote. It's almost a plea to my brothers and sisters to stop and smell the roses, so to speak.

YOUR REFLECTIONS

Write a letter to Mother Nature. You may want to express gratitude, wonder, awe or love... or even apologise to Her. Open your heart.

What emotions came up for you in this process? Did anything surprise you?

A CRY FOR HELP

This friction, it feels plain bad.
This friction, it makes me mad.
This friction wants total control.
This friction stops me getting on a roll.

This friction sparks a negative feeling.
This friction sends my emotions reeling.
This friction feels like spiritual privation.
This friction robs me of my motivation.

This friction sure ain't what I asked for.
This friction I've seen often times before.
This friction always raises its head.
This friction makes me feel brain dead.

This friction, it just rules my life.
This friction is my emotional strife.
This friction keeps me down way low.
This friction, oh Lord, help me find flow.

This friction, it can come and go.
This friction wants to put on a show.
This friction, is it a sign from above?
This friction denies me unconditional love.

This friction, it cheeses me off.
This friction is not a one-off.
This friction is a real part of me.
This friction, love it and set yourself free.

MY REFLECTIONS

Ever felt like life is just plain hard? Like you're dragging a heavy ball around with you? Like there's some invisible force or friction choking the smooth flow of life? And that despite your best efforts, you never really get the results you thought you would?

Good. It's not just me then!

My journey into the Shadow is about freedom and flow. It's about bringing to balance those unseen forces keeping me stuck in old patterns. The key to how to do this is in the last verse.

YOUR REFLECTIONS

List times in your life when you felt held back by some kind of friction.

If the friction that's holding you back had a shape or face or form, what would it be? Draw it here.

Thinking back to your examples of times of friction, how did this make you feel and how did you respond?

It may not feel like it at the time, but I believe in every moment there is a gift or benefit. Pick one friction example from the list above and explore here how this experience, however negative, benefitted you.

THE EDGE

It feels like I'm standing on the edge of a cliff.

I'm torn by two voices.
One says jump, relax, trust, have faith...
The other says don't be stupid, no one in their right mind would do that.

Why?

I look down. A metre below and as far as I can see are clouds, fluffy white and thick. Swirling, moving, like molten rock, but never clearing or rising.

What's below the clouds?
An abyss and all the terror it holds?
Or a Garden of Eden, lush, green and fertile, just a few centimetres below the clouds?

What should I do? Jump?
Don't be silly. But you can't stay still. No one does.
Move. Edge along the cliff at least. Shuffle. Get busy. Move. Only pussies stay still, my mind screams.

And so I shimmy sideways. And when I look down the clouds are there. Still. So I shuffle sideways some more, only faster this time. I look down again.

Still the clouds. I'm in a different position, tired from all the sideways moving. But nothing's changed.

Go on, jump...

MY REFLECTIONS

This is a story about life patterns. I have always defaulted to playing safe, part of the pact I made as a young boy. But I'm getting better at leaping. Yes, the leap is scary. Yes, you can fall. But gee, it's exhilarating. This book is one of my leaps.

I wrote this poem after a dream I had. And yes, it describes what happened in the early hours inside my mind... the cliff, the clouds, the fear, the edging along... then I jumped... and woke up before I found out what happened.

What do you do when you stand on the edge of your cliff?

YOUR REFLECTIONS

Identify three of your life patterns. Record them in the space below.

Next to each, explain why you feel you stick to the pattern.

→

→

→

Pick one pattern. Write a letter to it. Thank it for all it's done for you up to this point. Go deep. Tell it you love it and want to let it go.

IN HIDING

I hid from you all this time
Down in the hole, curled up and safe.
It was easier in there, comfortable
And my mind kept reminding me so.

I hid from the world and suffered in silence
Kept down, guilted, squashed low.
It did become easier to deal with the pain
And then the walls came up, strong and high.

I hid from you for half my life
Knowing there was more, pushing me away.
My heart never gave up, patient always,
And then the walls started to crumble.

I hid from my heart for far too long
Simpler, sweeter, safer to block its power.
My love turned to stone just to cope,
Until I saw my true magnificence.

And the world suddenly changed...

THE SHIFT

Transition
To
Love.

Give
Love.

Share
Love.

Help
Others
With
Love.

Heal
With
Love.

Just
Love.

MY REFLECTIONS

During a busy day, I paused to just be. And a funny thing happened. I realised I had shifted. Old triggers were nowhere near as spikey. As I reflected on the previous few hours, I realised things didn't piss me off nearly as much. Even better, I could identify and acknowledge my mood with greater ease, and without guilt. I asked why and these two poems came one after the other. My inner world had come out of 'hiding'. And I was more open to the power of love. It was a nice feeling...

YOUR REFLECTIONS

What does a shift, or emergence from spiritual 'hiding', mean to you? Write or draw your response here. Go deep...

YOU, THE ARTIST

Live like an artist where nothing makes sense,
Let go and be, just allow and feel less tense.

When stuck in your head trying to work it out,
It fractures your energy and lets chaos shout.

Notice how you're feeling and be true to yourself,
Let go and relax, the universe then offers help.

If you force it and make all the ducks line up,
You'll feel the pain, and things will fuck up.

Be open and talk to your guides all the more,
Feel the energy and love without keeping score.

Think like an artist, love you and be free,
It will all come together, just watch and see.

There's a whole new field of energy awaiting to explore,
Just go with it, feel it, your life is so much more.

Be an artist, don't try to run away,
Feel into it and let love, your heart lead the way.

MY REFLECTIONS

A couple of decades ago, the chiropractor I was seeing had a big wall poster, *How to Be an Artist* by SARK. Google it. It's beautiful.

I strive every day to live more like an artist. Wish I was more successful at it. Life does get in the way. Old patterns, the stuff still in my Shadow, influence me. But I'm working on it. And the message in this poem is a constant theme for me… open up, let go, trust…

There is freedom in creativity, in being an artist, if only we'd allow it more in our lives.

YOUR REFLECTIONS

What art or creativity is there lurking in you, just waiting to come out?

No one's watching... NOW... write it... draw it... sing it... dance it... just do it, NOW.

What came up for you in this exercise? How can you change things? Are you willing to change to allow more creativity in your life?

JUST

A clear mind
A calm heart
Not a deadline in sight,
Just be.

A still mind
An open heart
Nowhere need be,
Just me.

An empty mind
A big soft heart
Nothing to do,
Just see.

A free mind
A slowing heart
No expectation or judgement
Just be me.

FEAR

I don't know what to do.
I need help.
It will fail.
No one will like it.
What if it doesn't work.
Others do it way better.
Look how good they are.
You might look foolish.
You'll embarrass yourself.
This has never worked for me.
Small.
Less than.
Not worthy.
This and other bullshit
bounces around in my head.

MY REFLECTIONS

Examine again what goes on in your mind. When I was in stillness one day, I listened to my inner voice again and *Just* came to me. I wrote it and put my pen down. For some reason, out of nowhere, a wave of despair washed over me. It didn't make sense. I wrestled with it awhile. Then I let go and allowed the feelings to flow. For some reason, behind the despair was fear. I let it all come out and felt better when that energy was released through *Fear*.

YOUR REFLECTIONS

What's going on in your mind right now? Be honest. Don't judge. Write it here. Let it out...

Is there anything about you that hasn't been loved that you need to look at more closely? Explore this in words or pictures here...

IT LAUGHS AND SNEERS

The fear of returning to work you no longer love.
It sits with you, always there, knocking away.
The fear of doing what you don't want to do.
No matter how hard you try, still it holds sway.

It nags you.
Reminds you.
Teases you.
Controls you.

And it sits in your gut wanting not to move.
Everyone else enjoys their life.
But you fight and kick and scream and no one hears.
It's still just there, not going away.

Everything's okay, there's nothing to fear.
Why then does the mind laugh and sneer?
The joke repeats and shrinks you just so.
Another week to endure, fast I hope it will go.

MY REFLECTIONS

We spend about a third of our lives at work. How do you feel about your job/career? Is it a source of joy? Do you dread it? Are you bored by it? Resigned to being stuck in it? Or is your work a source of inspiration?

I asked myself these questions and the words poured out. Sure, it might have been a bad day. But the words also caused me to look deeper at my work life and what really sparks joy for me. If this triggers you, even a little, it might be time to look at your work and, for all the time and effort you put into it, make some changes so it's a positive, energising part of your life, not a drain. This takes some courage. Good luck!

YOUR REFLECTIONS

How do you feel, honestly, about your work or career? Respond here... a word dump, a poem, a drawing, a letter to your boss or favourite client, a photo collage of your feelings. Respond to how you feel about your work, just be honest with yourself.

TO THE LOUD VOICE IN MY HEAD

Fuck off you judgmental creep!
The truth is...
You are magnificent.
You are valuable.
You are a spark of life.
Such a powerful and divine being.
Much loved, unconditionally, warts and all...

IGNORE IT

Ignore your heart, listen to your mind
And be empty and frustrated all the time.
Ignore your mind, listen to your heart
And be fulfilled, warm, at peace from the start.
Ignore love, listen to your ego
And stay on that wheel to never let go.

RELEASE YOUR GENIUS

The energy has shifted.
Feel clear. Fresh. Excited.
Why the change?
Just go with the flow.
Open up. Allow. Relax and let Spirit in.
Greatness is never forced, it comes with ease.
Allow your greatness to come through.
Open.
Have confidence it will all be okay. It will.
Resistance blocks. Feel into it. When free, flow comes.
Flow. Allow. Relax.
Your genius then comes to the surface.

MY REFLECTIONS

These poems are a raw, honest and uncomfortable look at the thoughts pinging around in my head. Written several weeks apart, they show that I'm a work in progress. There are parts of my Shadow Self that I still need to look at and love. And then there are times I feel inspired, uplifted, free. And give myself a pep talk, which is what the last poem is. And then it seems I go back on the rollercoaster.

If you're silently agreeing with me right now because you can relate, thank you, I'm not the only rollercoaster rider here! These poems encourage you to keep looking, keep digging and keep shining a light on your Shadow.

YOUR REFLECTIONS

Do you judge others? Be honest. List examples below.

How or when do you judge yourself?

If you were to give yourself a pep talk, what would you say?

YOU FREAK

Shine, shine your light
Let it out for the world to see.
Live, live your life
It's really okay to just be.

They'll say, Go on, work hard, be a hit
Don't listen, that's about them
Follow it and you feel like shit
It's what they want, not your spirit in the end.

So be you in this very moment
You weird fuckin' freak.
Be strange and different
The world needs you to speak.

Those true will stay by you
Be there right at your side
Others will drift off, move away
With the real you, there's no need to hide.

So that pain of being true to you
It's there inside to help see you through.
They won't know or even understand
Welcome weirdo freak, great to meet you.

MY REFLECTIONS

Secret confession... I feel different. A freak. An outlier. Why? I don't know, just feels like I'm built different, as my teenage sons would say. If you too feel a little weird, welcome aboard, great to have you with us.

This poem is about others' expectations of us and our silent scream to be free, to be ourselves, in all our weirdness. There are many pressures on us to conform... from family, from work, from friends, from society. So much so it's easy to lose ourselves, our REAL selves. When I asked why it had to be like this, here's what came.

YOUR REFLECTIONS

In what ways are you...

| The same/similar to family and friends? | Different to family and friends? |

Which of these two lists is closer to the REAL you? Why?

In what areas of your life are you expected to conform to others' beliefs?

How do you expect others to conform to your beliefs?

What parts of you need to be loved more?

THE SEARCH

In search of balance
In search of peace
In search of happy
In search of release.

In search of truth
In search of care
In search of harmony
In search from despair.

In search of calm
In search of free
In search of joy
In search of me.

In search of healing
In search of the key
In search of the answer
It's a search to be me.

MY REFLECTIONS

Diving into my Shadow Self feels like a never-ending search. As much as I've tried – and I've tried a lot – the more we look outside of ourselves, the further we get from the answers we need. All the courses, webinars, seminars, podcasts, books, healings and reading can be a distraction. I know, I've done them all. And drugs, alcohol and partying are not the answer either. All of these are temporary pain relievers. We can dull the pain, gloss over it... but unless we love it and find a way to embrace it, it comes back again and again. Your journey in the Shadow Self is a search for the real you.

YOUR REFLECTIONS

What are you searching for in your life, honestly?

SMALL MOMENTS

It's fleeting, these moments of peace.
Too often 'they' return and take over.

Self-doubt. Small. Contracted. Less than. Stay safe.

Why are they always there, just a silent moment away from taking over?

You need to do more. Be more.
That's not good enough.
If you let go, bad shit might happen.

Don't feel good now, you don't deserve it.
Why do you judge yourself so much?

On and on it drones, never do I hear it say...

Just for today, listen to that other voice...

You are enough.
You are good.
You can do it.
You know the answer.
The way forward.
You are the light.

Let it shine. Just for today.
Just in this moment.
And then the next.

MY REFLECTIONS

One day when I was still, I listened to my mind chatter. Scary. It was almost all negative. Which troubled me enough to write this. Thank goodness, every day is not like that. But this episode and the words here are enough encouragement for me to keep going on my inward journey. Yep, there's still work to do. More parts of me that I'm still to love.

YOUR REFLECTIONS

Once again, in a moment of stillness, take an inventory of the thoughts you've had over the last several hours. List them here...

What surprised you about your mind chatter?

Did it bring up any thoughts about parts of you that haven't yet been loved?

NOT TWO

Pressure stifles me
Busy-ness addles my mind.
Too many thoughts rob my peace.
Rush harms.
'Too much' takes away.

When I sit.
When I allow.
When I be...
Then I connect to me.

Not two, caught in the 3D.
But one with all.
At peace. Alive. Free.

Not two, one...

The 3D wants two.
I choose to slow. To allow. To be.
And stay as one.

I AM ENOUGH

I am a writer
I am a creator
I am a healer
I am a leader
I am a way-shower
I am not of this world
I am magnificent at what I do
I am love
I am all
I am me...
And that is enough

MY REFLECTIONS

What is it about you or your life you have trouble accepting? These two poems are my yin/yang. *Not Two* reveals parts of me I have disliked that are lurking in my Shadow, still. *I Am Enough* is the declaration of my true self. One of the things I find difficult is to not get dragged back into the 3D and all its trivialities. It frustrates me when I see others default to the meaningless, or when they make a big deal out of things that don't really matter. The self-generated negativity... the arguments, jealousy, gossip are so easy to get sucked into. And if you have a busy day, it's even easier. It seems my life's work is to stay as one, not separate in the 3D... and... to be my own version of 'I Am'.

YOUR REFLECTIONS

What aspects of you/your persona do others point out?

What do you feel deeply about you? These can be either or both positive and negative qualities. Record your responses here...

LET ME FLOW

Hold on tight in this rollercoaster life
If I grip real hard, it'll protect me from strife.

When I cling to the outcome, it brings it right here?
The cars, the house, the awards, yep, just be clear.

They say to set your goals and hold them there, bro
They don't tell you the striving won't make it so.

Because the more you hold tight and try to control
The harder it is to feel your true soul.

The outcomes others see they think bring great pride
But the reality hits, to get there, part of you died.

The outcome they tell you makes you happy, so think it
Until you realise how empty are the trinkets.

Look deep within now and let the others cling tight
For you to be free is well worth the fight.

Let go, be still and struggle all the less
When you relax, you flow and are open to be blessed.

MY REFLECTIONS

I've never been a huge goal setter. Maybe it's just that I hid from or wanted to avoid the disappointment of not achieving what I'd written down and committed to. Yes, I get it… aim for the stars and you might hit the moon and all that stuff. I just never really connected to it. To me, goals feel like force, or like they limit the outcome. I'm not sure, I just know that goals and I don't really get along and never have. As I pondered why, these words came to me.

YOUR REFLECTIONS

Are you a formal goal setter? Do you use the SMART acronym or whatever else is fashionable these days? Or are you more a go-with-the-flow type? How has goal setting or going-with-the-flow worked out for you? There is no right or wrong here. But have a look and see what feels right for you.

Record your thoughts here...

AM I THE ONLY ONE?

I fear being exposed.
I fear they'll find out.
I fear I'll miss the deadline.
I fear the guilt that comes with expectations.

Am I the only one who fears this way?
Honestly, Spirit, I want more.

More...

Peace.
Calm.
Confidence.
Abundance.
Time.
Love.

Maybe I'm just like everyone else...

All my fears.
My guilt.
My anxiety.

Or maybe they just make me me...
And it's time to love them.
And accept me?

MY REFLECTIONS

Working with the Shadow, or any kind of spiritual work in fact, can be lonely. Over time, you feel separate from others. And as much as you don't want to, you look at others caught in the 3D and, fleetingly, want to be back there. It's easier to be asleep and remain on the hamster wheel of life… get through the working week to the weekend, have a BBQ with friends, do the family chores, go out… and then do it all again next week. That's easy! Looking deeper at you and your life? That's hard because the internal disruption is never comfortable. Or easy. And it eventually shows in your outer reality too.

Pretty soon, as others continue to stay asleep, it can feel like you are the only one going through the struggle. Friends drop away. You don't see family as much. Things that interested you before no longer hold your attention. The thing is, once you start the journey into the Shadow, it's almost impossible to go back to the 'old' you. Stay true to you and keep going. You are worth it.

YOUR REFLECTIONS

Stop. Get still. Listen.

What do you fear most? What do you want more of? What do you need to love about you more? What comes up?

A BRAVE YOUNG MAN

A brave young man followed his heart today,
A brave young man showed his parents the way.
A brave young man defied their expectations,
A brave young man rejected all solicitations.

A brave young man pushed through the hurt,
A brave young man gave up his shirt.
A brave young man chose a new path,
A brave young man followed his heart.

A brave young man was strong enough to cry,
A brave young man was able to say goodbye.
A brave young man found the peace of the dove,
A brave young man saw unconditional love.

A brave young man felt the energy shift,
A brave young man listened to his God-given gifts.
A brave young man wanted to start anew,
A brave young man left behind what he knew.

A brave young man chose a new path,
A brave young man with the strength of a staff.
A brave young man followed his heart today,
A brave young man's life is now underway.

More power to you, Nate, my brave young man...

MY REFLECTIONS

I wrote this the day after our youngest son retired from a promising football career at the age of 16. The pain was multi-level. He would no longer be the trophy child, it was the end of long sport weekends with the kids, the end of him and I doing stuff together while travelling the state and the world for football. The training, the games, the preparation, the riding every pass and tackle... it ended right there.

In truth, there was a lot of pressure on him to continue playing but he stayed true to himself. He knew in his heart of hearts it was time to stop. It was a bittersweet moment. The thing that really hurt was the realisation that had it been my 16-year-old self, immersed full-on into trophy child/parent pleasing mode, I think I would have kept playing and told myself it was okay. I was awed by my son's bravery and the lesson he taught me. And yes, I wrote this with tears running down my cheeks.

YOUR REFLECTIONS

List down things you have done in your life merely out of obligation.

How did you feel about it afterwards?

Have you ever pushed your kids into things they didn't really want to do? If you don't have kids, were you ever pushed into something you didn't want to do? Either way, looking back now, what emotions come up for you?

What other deeply buried emotions does this poem bring up? From your own upbringing perhaps?

THIS EXISTENCE

*Everyone else it seems is happy. I'm miserable. Bored. Down.
Depressed. Pissed off with where I'm at. Worst thing is, I've ALWAYS
felt this way.
Why me?*

*I just want to be happy and free. At peace. Live a carefree life.
I want to be able to roll with the punches and still be happy.
Not the fake-happy you show the world. Real-happy you feel.
I want to be proud of who I am.
I hate being me... so limited, restricted, small. This is hard.
It feels like I'm in a big hole.*

*Life has always felt this way... I've always looked outward to solve it...
new career, pushed the feelings down and locked them away so they
can't hurt me and the world can't see them.
Why does it feel so bad, so hard?
This is an awful existence... no peace, no love, no hope, no joy.
I can't focus on the now. I have to protect
This is an awful existence
Too often I feel like there's
No peace. No love. No joy. No hope.*

Focus on the now? No way.
I have to protect myself from the future. I must be prepared. So I have to think about that. Or... I must punish myself. Drag up the past. The mistakes. The pain. Re-live it all over, again and again.
What I should have said.
What I should have done.
What I should have felt.
How I should have reacted.

Always I was lesser. Could have. Should have... Done more. Less. Better. The opposite to what I actually did.
It wasn't good enough.
I wasn't good enough.
I'm not good enough.

This pain. This frustration. This guilt.
It hurts. It's horrible. It's no way to live.
I want to feel free.

MY REFLECTIONS

This is me at my most vulnerable, deep in the Shadow. There's much (all?) pain here. Shadow work can feel like this. The pain is acute. Releasing this energy by shining a light on it, speaking it out, feeling it, acknowledging it, loving it as part of me is where the work comes in. These are the steps to freedom.

YOUR REFLECTIONS

Look back to a time when you felt down. What comes up for you? Maybe it's now? Whatever you felt then/now, be honest. Write it down. In verse. In free writing. A nonsensical blurt. Write it down now.

THOUGHTS

Love
Innocence
Feeling
Heart
Emotion
People trapped
Feel weak
Return to you
Let go
Slow down
Tears unshed
Listen to your heart
Divine
Heart catch up
Mind rules
Mind acknowledge the heart
Ignore the heart
Sadness
Nervousness
New sensations
Uncomfortable
Be exposed
Feel the energy
Aligned
Suppress
Empty
Searching
Run from
Protection
Worthy
Not small
Blazing angel
Energy

MY REFLECTIONS

Our world of duality. One day I just wanted to write and only single words, at most short phrases, came out. The weirdest thing was, on this day, a mixture of words came… 'good' ones as well as 'bad' ones. Normally when I write it's one or the other. Why it was like this, I have no idea. These words just poured out.

I believe we are always a mixture of thoughts, both positive and negative. And often it can feel a little nonsensical, like this poem. I believe there is beauty in this chaos too…

YOUR REFLECTIONS

As you embark on your current journey inward, what are you feeling? Complete a word dump here. Don't edit or filter it, just write what comes... the good, the bad, the ugly, the unspeakable... everything.

AM I BROKEN?

When I'm honest about how I really feel
The pain wells up, it's raw and real.
Any happiness I felt was fleeting, a mere token
The truth here, world, is I feel fucking broken.

But as I go on pushing harder, striving to get in the life race
All this hamster wheel running to achieve, to save face.
That smiling fragile boy never had a fighting chance
To feel love and be free, get out of the heavy ego trance.

And here we are fifty years down the track
All I've done is open the real me, just a crack.
I want my light to shine but don't yet know how
All I was taught was to perform, here kid, take another bow.

It was never me, just a shell of the ego perception
Go on, smile now, kid, it's an important community reception.
To linger in this trance thinking it was sane
Was but a lie, when all along I was in deep pain.

Where to now you've seen the truth, and it hurts
I take solace in the divine me, I now see in spurts.
For there is more pain to feel, more tears yet to shed
Spirit, lead me to my heart and get me out of my head.

MY REFLECTIONS

Yep, the journey into the Shadow Self is not comfortable. This poem explains why. You have to face all the things about you that you don't want to. Things about your upbringing, your relationships... and about you. You can't love all of you if you don't see all of you. It's important work. Keep going. You're worth it.

YOUR REFLECTIONS

Have you ever felt broken? Or at least damaged? Hopefully it's not just me!! Write what comes when you examine this negative phase of the journey within...

I NEEDED THIS

*So this is a nice writer's creative nest
A place to still, unwind, and at last rest.
The thud and pop of the ever-present waves,
The way to open my heart it subtly paves.*

*The rush, the hustle, the pressure
Of normal busy life, it grinds me to lesser
So happy to be here in this breezy place
Time to slow, open my sacred heart space.*

*As the cool wind caresses me just so
I gaze at the surf, it's hard to feel low.
To be present and connected to the now
Is my quest, Spirit, this week show me how.*

*The human sounds of fun, laughter are light
Drift in on the wind, helps me give up the fight.
Now it's time to leave that usual busy-like trance
This week I'm closed for my spiritual maintenance.*

MY REFLECTIONS

The beach is my happy place. It always has been. From the family holidays as a kid to the present-day walk on the sand in the morning, a body surf during the day, or just sitting and watching the sky and waves change colour as the sun dips below the horizon.

One time we went away for a week to our favourite beach locale. The first afternoon, after the unpacking and familiarisation one usually does, I sat out the back and listened to the gentle mixture of the natural and human world. I breathed in the sea air real deep and smiled. And these words came to me.

YOUR REFLECTIONS

Where do you go for your 'spiritual maintenance'? What about this place appeals to you?

Bucket list time! What 20 places would you like to visit but haven't?

1.
2.
3.
4.
5.
6.
7.
8.
9.
10.

11.
12.
13.
14.
15.
16.
17.
18.
19.
20.

What has stopped you?

Think back to your favourite holiday as a kid. What was so memorable about it? What stops you from pursuing a similar experience as an adult? Is there something around holidays in your Shadow you need to shine a light on and love?

I AM OPEN TO

I am open to
New ways
Remembering the old
Guidance from Yeshua, Mother Mary, Archangel Michael
Letting go
Being still
Doing the Father's work
Being richly rewarded
Loving me unconditionally
Feeling worthy
Feeling peace
Feeling confident
Being whole
Living in my heart space
Speaking my truth
Finding my voice
Accepting help
Sharing love
Being vulnerable

MY REFLECTIONS

When I tap into the feelings I've squashed down in my Shadow – spirituality, vulnerability, art, being true to myself and speaking it in every moment – it makes me feel uncomfortable. This was an uncomfortable poem to write. Like all the others though, it had to come out because if we are to move on, we must be open to new things, always.

YOUR REFLECTIONS

What 'new ways' are you open to? Think in terms of your thoughts, your work, your creativity, your relationships, your family, your finances, your connection to Source... Examine all parts of your life and record what comes up.

SHE'S OKAY, I THINK

Got a problem... no worries, I know what to do,
It's okay, we got this, I know who we turn to.
We can pass it on, the solution's set, completely inescapable,
Fear not, it's all okay, because she's just so damn capable.

Can we lean on her, just a little more, get her to help out?
Of course, it's natural and easy, just give her a quick shout.
She'll do it, it's all good, this girl of ours, freely shapable,
Worry not now, it's done, the kid's so damn capable.

Let's ask her again, I'm sure it's fine, no doubt she's got this,
Good, we'll do it more, even if it's the whole long list.
And we know it'll be great, it's proven beyond debatable,
Yep, she's a shining light that girl, just so damn capable.

There's lots to do now, more help needed today, the most,
She's always there, and of her skills, I do so love to boast.
Because the world knows it's true, and darn near unshakeable,
That girl I love her so, because she's just so damn capable.

So I lean on her some more, just like I did in the past,
It's all good, she's fine, there's no need to even ask.
All along she's come through, completely true and trainable,
What a horrid cross she now bears, being so damn capable.

But we push on, the pattern's set, no need to even blink,
That winning smile, her busy life, did I ever stop to think?
I just assumed she'd be okay, that happy mask there, unshakeable,
Is she okay? I have no idea, I only see her... as so damn capable.

MY REFLECTIONS

One morning during a small group spiritual clearing session, we were reflecting on our upbringing and how we raised our kids. A woman in the group described how, when she was ill and her kids were young, she had leaned on her eldest daughter for help. She told how great the girl was. One phrase stood out. *"She's always been so capable."* What's so wrong with that? This belief caused the woman to be blind to her daughter's illness later in life. She believed that because her daughter had always been 'okay', she would always be, well, 'okay'. It was a touching moment and a painful revelation for her, to know her daughter was not okay. It also caused me to think about where I had failed to really 'see' my kids. This is what came to me.

YOUR REFLECTIONS

What scares you the most when you think about those you love? Losing them? Not seeing them? Not helping them when they need it? What exactly?

Why do these things spike fear in you?

What might these feelings reveal about your Shadow Self?

THE GUILT OF RELIGION

Tackling the guilt of religion is my toughest ask yet
More pain to come, more tears to shed, more angst, I bet

Why did man create this thing, a controlling, unyielding beast?
Is it just to keep our spirit down so we gently feel the least?

For me it seems just so, always there a dank dark cloak,
Pinning my soul, holding me back, stopping me going for broke.

I just wish it wasn't, but such is this, a path to my deeper pain
To look at it, to love it some, it's the only way to sane.

When I drop the cloak, I'll feel exposed, ever naked in this hour,
Let it fall, love it still, let me reclaim my birthright power.

It brings regrets, that funny feel, deep inside my gut,
Because I see it now, how much it did keep my heart real shut.

The good Catholic Boy, the little one who swallowed it down whole,
The battle's now, to love him still, it's victory for my soul.

What a strange and curious thing is this heavy religious cloak
To take it off, to love it now and let it go afloat.

It's the only way to accept myself and break its chains on me
Love that religious good boy, do it now, you'll be amazed at what you see.

Keep going on your journey now, it's not time to pull up stumps,
Feel the pain, give the love, and soon you'll be rid of that gut-churning lump.

I hereby acknowledge my strict religious past,

I love it now, thank it and release it so,

Goodbye my friend, on you go, you were never meant to last.

MY REFLECTIONS

As a 'good Catholic boy', I've carried much guilt all my life. I didn't realise how much until I started looking, really looking. The truth is, it permeated just about every area of my life. I've given religion the flick, permanently. I now have a deep spirituality, deeper than I ever did in my religious days. I read the Bible regularly and have a particular affinity with Psalm 23. This poem is acknowledging and shedding that religious baggage. It's time to be free.

YOUR REFLECTIONS

What guilt do you harbour? Bring it out here... words, pictures, a dance, music... love it and release it...

THE POWER OF YOUR WORDS

Words based in love
Words that are felt.
Words that come from inside
Words that touch the soul.

Words that speak to the heart
Words that awaken a life.
Words that uplift
Words that light the way.

Words that go deep
Words that spark action.
Words that come from above
Words that help others feel love.

Words that change thoughts
Words that flow with ease.
Words that move mountains
Words from within, that touch Man.

THE REAL YOU

Listen to your heart
That gentle pure voice
That hides beneath
Your strong urgent mind.

It's the real you,
Open to its message
Let the wisdom flow
And be free.

It's okay to be vulnerable
It's safe to be exposed
It's about being okay with fear
It's about the real you.

Urgent is the mind
Gentle is the heart.
One is made up
The other is you, my friend.

MY REFLECTIONS

The words we speak to others and to ourselves hold enormous power. When they come from the heart, we speak with a gentle strength. When they come from the mind, what we speak can be spikey, urgent and needy. Where do your words come from most of the time? The thing is, every time I think I've got this nailed I catch myself saying words from the mind. Frustrating. But I'm getting better!

YOUR REFLECTIONS

Monitor your thoughts. Do you judge others? Give examples.

Why do you think this is the case?

How does it feel to admit it?

Love that part of your Shadow. What words would you say to it?

THE CAGE

I'm running fast all day surrounded by a cage
Nowhere to go everywhere to get, feel the surging rage.
The motion just won't stop, it drives me to despair
Tingling inside hello old me, welcome back, I just don't care.

Tis the way I've always been, my poker face in place
Push it down, run around, feel like a basket case.
Drive on, shoulder to the load, this is getting real
So busy, so alone, so worked up, no idea how I feel.

Numb inside but a bright smile to keep the world at peace
All I want is to run away and leave these awful streets.
Is there hope, is there hope, is there even possibility?
Don't be silly, boy, busy yourself in all that responsibility.

Fleeting moments of sweet rest at last, it's here
No it's not yours, silly boy, that happiness it did appear.
What's the answer then to this lifelong horrid shit show
No idea, me lad, but I'm sure it's better over home.

One more breath, then let's hope it all changes real fast
Because I can't take much more of this, it's all about my past.
Let go, they say, smile bright, turn over a brand-new page
No it's not you, sucker punch, you're still trapped in your fucking cage.

MY REFLECTIONS

A journey into the Shadow Self is about honesty. This is raw and honest. And painful. Yep, it was a pretty bad day. I was authentic, however, when I expressed how I was feeling. And that felt good. No need for a mask. No need to be anything for anyone else other than what I was feeling, trapped in a cage. The next day I felt really good, like the cage had disappeared.

So dive in, be real, raw and authentic. You might be surprised what comes up and how liberating it feels.

YOUR REFLECTIONS

In what way/s does your life feel like a cage?

If 'cage' is an inappropriate metaphor for you, pick another and write how it influences your life.

THE STORY OF MY LIFE

Oh, how I shone, so bright and high, there for the world to see,
Those awards, trophies and smiles buried the real soft me?
Or was I simply on stage doing their praiseworthy dance,
So everyone could grin and clap, stuck in their 3D trance?

A willing participant was I, a new award to strive and win,
And dive right in I did, coming second a mortal sin.
Carry on, mask of praise stuck firmly to my face,
Get out there, mate, go hard, win that bloody race.

When you do, they will see how great we truly are,
Shucks, it's nothing folks, move over, on to my next star.
Love you heaps, young man, for all you do and achieve,
And we pray in these bright awards, you keep on and do believe.

On I push, a slave to their rules, no need to even thinketh,
Keep striving now, go on pal, grab that next empty trinket.
Do it lad, get out there, have a crack and play your part,
It matters not however, son, if you never listen to your heart.

With these awards and status, you're the perfect man to see,
Smile on, appearances up, there's no other way to be.
You've done it well, we counted on you, now look on you and smile,
Even if you've been crushed, you've done good, our perfect trophy child.

MY REFLECTIONS

On the same day I wrote *She's okay, I think*..., I had another revelation of how I'd been a 'trophy child' all my life. In that spiritual clearing session, I saw how just about everything I had ever done had been passed through the trophy filter. All the people pleasing. All the doing the right thing. It's an emotional prison. This poem is my release from jail, no longer the trophy for anyone. Freedom feels good!

YOUR REFLECTIONS

What does this bring up for you?

How are you a trophy to others? How do you feel about it?

How have you made others a trophy?

What can you do to change this?

What parts of you do you now have to love?

THE HARD-HEARTED MAN

He smiled gently as he opened his innocent young heart
Soft and mushy, it did feel right from the very start.

Then confusion set in, the energy not reciprocated
She smiled alright but the young boy felt manipulated.

It didn't seem right, fear set in, but he didn't disappoint
Instead closed off his heart and thought, what's the bloody point?

And the walls went up as the other kids too made fun
A soft gentle heart is dangerous here, quick, shut down and run.

A pattern was set, a need then for heart protection
All through his life he ran, never giving real affection.

The feminine was dark and something to be feared
Forever in his energy was the deep pain seared.

And suspicious of others was the energy at play
Held him back, it has done to this very day.

Until along came a wise, skilled and caring old soul
Made him feel safe, and repaired that dark hole.

And open up and trust the hardened man did
Let go of his fear, he lifted his heart lid.

Life became clearer, easier, more free
But deep regret he felt when this he did see.

The soft loving heart, however, could not be denied
Trust others became safe, when before he never tried.

A hug, a smile, a gentle touch without expectation
Was new to the man, weird, and a foreign sensation.

As his heart walls came down, he tried this some more
Love is beautiful, yes I'm here, ready to explore.

At last it felt safe to let go, reach out to others
No worry any more of his wishes being smothered.

Each day is another step in the right direction
A caress, an eye twinkle, more okay with genuine affection.

And so here we are, this story now to impart
Open up, it's okay, strong man… with the beautiful soft heart.

MY REFLECTIONS

This is about the invisible forces that control our lives – in my case, the Dark Feminine. When I finally discovered this part of my Shadow, I first felt VERY uncomfortable, then very vulnerable, and then very small.

This poem tells my story, lays bare my struggles. My hope is it will prise something open in you, something you don't want to see or feel. One thing I can assure you is, it's okay. And even when you face these tough realisations, you'll be okay.

YOUR REFLECTIONS

How open do you feel your heart is? Give a percentage.

What has led you to close your heart off, to build walls and avoid intimacy? Fear of the feminine? Fear of the masculine? Some other fear?

How have these fears ruled your life?

It's time to love this part of you. What would it mean to accept this in you?

MY ATTACHMENTS

It stuck like Velcro
When I rip it off
It makes that harsh
Scratching sound, yuck

It's been there as long
As I can remember
Holding me in check
Keeping me stuck again

Something's burned inside
For how long I know not
But it's been there, a
Perpetual stone around my neck

What is it that's held me back
So long all these years
It's the Velcro stuff
Hey there, attachment

To the outcome, the result
To the control, the safety
To the looking good, the mask
To the known, the certainty

To the relationships, smooth
To the things, look
To the comfort, ease
To the niceties, aaah

To the accolades, go me
To the image, my fake self
To the smiles, the pretend
To the time, another deadline

Attachment has been
That rock around my neck
Holding me back
Robbing me of peace.

To be uncertain is freedom
To be unsure is liberty
To be open is trust
To be light, unattached is life

Attachment to all that
To people, to outcomes
Is but attempted control
Control is death

For my soft heart at least...

MY REFLECTIONS

Just before the close of the year of years that was 2020, I received a download about the need to let go of my attachments. What attachments? Turns out I have quite a few. Two days after the message from Spirit, these words came to me. This was another uncomfortable revelation. I thought I'd let go of them already, but I guess it's a case of the old red flag: "I've already dealt with that." Most people recognise when they hear those words the person saying them is trying to convince themselves the issue doesn't affect them anymore. The one who hears these words, however, feels the truth... "I've already dealt with that" is a cover for *it still pisses me off and I don't want to revisit it*. Keep an eye out for it, it's lurking there!

YOUR REFLECTIONS

What in your life are you attached to? Make a list.

Which of these attachments are you prepared to let go of? What would it mean to your life to do this?

What surprised you about your responses to attachments?

WELCOME, MY DARKEST THOUGHTS

Resisting increases their power
Squashing them gives them strength Rejecting them fuels their force
Yes, neglect makes my negatives come back to bite me and rule my life.

How then can I manage
My emotions and those
Parts of me that aren't the slightest bit comfortable?

If darkness gives them grunt?

Let's start by acknowledging
Yes, there is anxiety there
Then I can greet it
Hello anxiety, welcome, nice to see you again.

And then... instead of
Ignoring, rejecting or punishing
I open my heart and give
Anxiety a big warm cuddle

And I feel anxiety's power
Dissipate in my love
It's a process, see, to deal
With those parts we push away

They rule me without me knowing
They control my thoughts without me thinking
They run my mind, like a dark autopilot
My Shadow Self, hello,
Time to shine some light on you and accept you

Acknowledge
Welcome
Open my heart
Hug anxiety

That's better.

Now let's look
Some more...
There is fear there

Hello fear, welcome
And on it goes
As I shine the
Light on my
Shadow Self...

MY REFLECTIONS

To finish the book, I wanted to share the process I use to shine the light on my Shadow Self. As the poem describes, whenever I feel a spikey emotion, instead of ignoring it or squashing it because it's painful, like I have done most of my life, I now acknowledge it, open my heart to it, tell it I love it and give it a big cuddle. I even open my arms wide and bring the emotion to my chest. Try it sometime... it might just work.

YOUR REFLECTIONS

Take a deep breath. What do you feel exists deep within your Shadow Self that you've yet to acknowledge? Don't judge, just acknowledge it. Make a list.

When the time feels right, for each of these, go through the process. Acknowledge the feeling... open your heart to it... welcome it... give it a hug... and let that emotions dissipate in the love of your heart space. Record here what comes up for you.

Conclusion

You've made it to the end, congratulations. The reading, the reflecting, the responding with pen in hand requires effort. Getting to this point shows you are a rare and advanced soul. Well done. You have my deepest admiration.

A few more thoughts from me to consider as you continue your journey into the Shadow Self...

You are not perfect. You will continue to make mistakes. And you will feel, at times, like you are getting nowhere. That's not true. Keep going. I want you to know you are okay as you are. You are not broken. Your ego might tell you that you are, but you're not. And you don't owe anyone anything. There will be times in the weeks and months ahead when you want to shut up shop and go back to the 'old' ways of being busy, rushing about and ignoring your heart. When you feel this happening, suspend your self-judgement. Be still. Drop into your heart space. Breathe. Feel. Get back to you.

One thing I know for certain is this: When you change you, you change the world. Your family feels it and is elevated. When you've done the internal work, you send higher vibrations out into the field. Naturally you get higher vibrations back, which brings different life results. You are worth the effort.

It reminds me of the parable of the woman walking along the beach and seeing a lot of starfish washed up high and dry on the sand. There were hundreds of them. She started picking them up and throwing them one by one back into the sea. A jogger stopped when he drew level with her and asked what she was doing, saying it was futile to try and save them

Conclusion

all. The woman smiled as she picked up another one and threw it into the sea. "Saved that one," she said.

This book and your journey into your Shadow Self are just like that. We change our world one 'starfish' at a time.

I would also encourage you to take the time to develop your creativity. 'I'm not creative' is not a valid response. Yes, you are, you've just ignored that part of you. I'm not saying you are Mozart or Rembrandt or Taylor Swift, but you are a creative being. When you tap into this part of you – through writing, singing, painting, dancing, acting and more – you connect to the God Source within. This is where your freedom begins. If you can't do your chosen creative thing every day, do it every second day. Just begin. A new world awaits.

You've started something life-changing with this book. It's time to bring even more light to your Shadow Self. Love every part of you.

Good luck on the journey…

Steve Vincent

Final thought...

"And I pray that he would unveil within you the unlimited riches of his glory and favour until supernatural strength floods your innermost being with his divine might and explosive power."

- Ephesians 3:16 (TPT)

Acknowledgements

To everyone who's helped me on this journey, thank you. Naming names is always fraught with the danger of leaving someone out. That said, here goes…

I'd like to thank all those beautiful souls who've helped crack the lid on my once very closed heart. To Donna, SJ and Adam, Marie, Peter, Grace, Warren and Will, my spiritual gym buddies Christine, Max, Fiona, Sam and Noelene. To Emily, Rae and the incredible team at Gowor International Publishing, who helped shape this project. Your wisdom and belief elevated it to a level I didn't foresee. Thank you. To my children, Eliza, Maddie, Isaac and Nate, thanks for choosing me as your lucky dad, it's been an honour and I look forward to seeing you grow even more. And last but not least to the beautiful soul I married, Jenny, who believed in me and loved me even when I didn't. You put up with my moods and down days, and stood beside me, behind me and in front of me when I needed you to.

Without any of you, this book would not have been possible. Thank you.

About the Author

Steve Vincent is a poet and spiritual teacher who helps people overcome their challenges and live their dharma.

A reclusive opacarophile, Steve's search for himself has stretched from the sands of the Sunshine Coast to the hot springs of New Zealand, to the Peruvian Amazon for ayahuasca ceremonies, and has included many an energetic healing online and in person, and long hours alone pondering the meaning of life.

Originally a high school teacher, faculty head and deputy principal then freelance journalist, copywriter, writing coach and marketing consultant, Steve Vincent Plummer's journey inwards has unlocked the pain of the human experience, which emerges in his words that are said to move women to tears and make men squirm. As a poet and spiritual teacher, he writes under his given names and presents internationally.

Steve lives on the Sunshine Coast and when not writing and leading groups, can be found at one of the beautiful local beaches communing with Mother Earth or gazing out to sea.

Find out more at www.stevevincentonline.com

www.ingramcontent.com/pod-product-compliance
Lightning Source LLC
Chambersburg PA
CBHW061132010526
44107CB00068B/2912